CHRIST OVER ALL

Christ Over All: Our Supreme Lord and Sufficient Savior

DESIGNED BY WEKREATIVE CO.
ISBN: 978-1-883973-19-3
PRINTED IN CHINA

COLOSSIANS 1

CHRIST OVER ALL

OUR SUPREME LORD AND SUFFICIENT SAVIOR

JOHN MACARTHUR

CONTENTS

INTRODUCTION

All Scripture is God-breathed and spiritually profitable for the salvation and sanctification of every believer. Every word of God is pure truth, living and life-giving, powerful and empowering.

For over half a century, I have lived daily with the Scripture in my hands and on my mind, preaching through all of the New Testament and many portions of the Old Testament from the pulpit of the church. This work in the Word has resulted in a full series of expository commentaries on each New Testament book, totaling thirty-four volumes, and a number of commentaries on various books of the Old Testament.

I am grateful for everyone who is willing to settle in and dig deep in reading a commentary. But only a few take on such an extensive journey, even though every aspect of the Scripture is life transforming. My desire, however, is for many to engage in such a pursuit because they will then experience the benefit and blessing of the deep dive into a biblical book.

I am certain when people have a taste of the riches of Bible exposition they will want more. So I thought we should give them less to develop the hunger for more.

What do I mean by less?

ONE CHAPTER. ONE MONUMENTAL CHAPTER.

So, that led to the development of this series, *The Great Chapters of the Bible.* This series focuses on key portions of Scripture that establish the foundational truths of the Christian faith. The current volume, adapted from *Colossians,* The MacArthur New Testament Commentary, examines the first chapter of Paul's epistle to the Colossians and his exaltation of Christ as our supreme Lord and sufficient Savior.

I believe that exposition of the great chapters of the Bible will lead many to desire to know the rest of each book and to experience the blessing of knowing the Scripture in its fullness.

01

THE GOSPEL TRUTH

COLOSSIANS 1:1–8

Paul, an apostle of Jesus Christ by the will of God, and Timothy our brother,

To the saints and faithful brethren in Christ *who are* at Colossae: Grace to you and peace from God our Father.

We give thanks to God, the Father of our Lord Jesus Christ, praying always for you, since we heard of your faith in Christ Jesus and the love which you have for all the saints; because of the hope laid up for you in heaven, of which you previously heard in the word of truth, the gospel which has come to you, just as in all the world also it is constantly bearing fruit and increasing, even as *it has been doing* in you also since the day you heard *of it* and understood the grace of God in truth; just as you learned *it* from Epaphras, our beloved fellow bond-servant, who is a faithful servant of Christ on our behalf, and he also informed us of your love in the Spirit. (1:1–8)

Scripture describes the gospel with several phrases. Acts 20:24 calls it "the gospel of the grace of God." Romans 1:9 designates it the "gospel of His Son," and 1 Corinthians 9:12 "the gospel of Christ." Romans 15:16 refers to it as "the gospel of God," 2 Corinthians 4:4 characterizes it as "the gospel of the glory of Christ," Ephesians 6:15 as "the gospel of peace," and Revelation 14:6 as the "eternal gospel."

The gospel is also described as the "word of truth" (Col 1:5), or the "message of truth" (Eph 1:13). Those descriptions have given rise to our common expression "the gospel truth." People use that phrase when they want to stress their sincerity, so that what they say will be believed.

Although people often use that expression flippantly, there is a real gospel truth. **Gospel** (v. 5) is the Greek word *euangelion*, from which we derive the English word *evangelize*. It literally means, "good news." It was used often in classical Greek to speak of the report of victory brought back from a battle. The gospel is the good news of Jesus' victory over Satan, sin, and death. It is also the good news that we, too, can triumph eternally over those enemies through Him.

First Corinthians 15:1–4 succinctly summarizes the historical content of the gospel: "Now I make known to you, brethren, the gospel which I preached to you, which also you received, in which also you stand, by which also you are saved, if you hold fast the word which I preached to you, unless you believed in vain. For I delivered to you as of first importance what I also received, that Christ died for our sins according to the Scriptures, and that He was buried, and that He was raised on the third day according to the Scriptures." The gospel is the good news that Jesus Christ died to provide complete forgiveness of sins and rose again that those who believe might live forever.

Such glorious, thrilling truth compels Christians to respond in several basic ways, all of which are noted by descriptive phrases using *gospel*. First, we should proclaim the good news, following the example of Jesus (Matt 4:23), the apostles, prophets, evangelists, teachers, and believers of all ages.

Second, we are to defend its veracity. Paul described himself as one "appointed for the defense of the gospel" (Phil 1:16). Peter told his readers to "make a defense to everyone who asks you to give an account for the hope that is in you" (1 Pet 3:15).

Third, we are to work hard for the advance of the gospel. Paul admonishes the Philippians to "[strive] together for the faith of the gospel" (Phil 1:27). The gospel demands of us discipline and strenuous effort.

Fourth, we are to pursue the fellowship we share with others who have believed the gospel. Devotion to the fellowship of the gospel characterized the early church (Acts 2:42). Paul often expressed his gratitude for those who had received the gospel (cf. Phil 1:3–5).

Fifth, we must be ready to suffer for the sake of the gospel. Paul exhorted Timothy, "Do not be ashamed of the testimony of our Lord or of me His prisoner; but join with *me* in suffering for the gospel" (2 Tim 1:8).

Sixth, we are to make sure that our lives do not hinder the gospel. Paul told the Corinthians that he would waive his right to be paid for his ministry rather than cheapen the message of the gospel (1 Cor 9:12).

Seventh, we must never be ashamed of the gospel. Paul said, "For I am not ashamed of the gospel, for it is the power of God for salvation to everyone who believes, to the Jew first and also to the Greek" (Rom 1:16).

Finally, we are to realize the gospel carries with it divine empowerment. Paul wrote to the Thessalonians, "Our gospel did not come to you in word only, but also in power and in the Holy Spirit" (1 Thess 1:5). The power of the gospel does not come from our cleverness or persuasiveness, but from the Holy Spirit.

This wonderful gospel is the reason for Paul's thanksgiving expressed in Colossians 1:3–8. Rejoicing at the report of their faith brought to him by Epaphras, the founder of the church at Colossae, he characteristically expresses thanks that the Colossians heard the gospel, and that it bore fruit in their lives.

Following the salutation in verses 1 and 2, Paul's words in verses 3–8 suggest seven aspects of the gospel: it is received by faith, results in love, rests in hope, reaches the world, reproduces fruit, is rooted in grace, and is reported by people. Before considering those aspects, let's take a brief look at the familiar terms of Paul's opening greeting that we find in his other epistles.

THE SALUTATION

Paul, an apostle of Jesus Christ by the will of God, and Timothy our brother,

To the saints and faithful brethren in Christ ***who are*** **at Colossae: Grace to you and peace from God our Father.** (1:1–2)

Following the practice of correspondence in the ancient world, Paul begins the letter with his name. Paul was the most important and influential person in history since our Lord Jesus Christ. His personality was the remarkable combination of a brilliant mind, an indomitable will, and a tender heart. Of Jewish ancestry, a "Hebrew of Hebrews" (Phil 3:5), he was a Pharisee (Phil 3:5). Paul was educated under Gamaliel (Acts 22:3), one of the leading rabbis of that time. He was also by birth a Roman citizen (Acts 22:28) and exposed to Greek culture in his home city of Tarsus. Such a background rendered him uniquely qualified to communicate the gospel in the Greco-Roman world. It was largely his efforts that transformed Christianity from a small Palestinian sect to a religion with adherents throughout the Roman Empire. The church would be blessed to have record of even one letter from such a man, let alone the thirteen found in the New Testament.

Lest anyone doubt his authority, Paul describes himself as **an apostle of Jesus Christ.** He is not simply a messenger, but an official representative of the One who sent him. What he writes in this letter is not merely his opinion, but God's authoritative Word.

Nor did he become an apostle through his own efforts. Neither was he nominated for the position by any human organization. Paul was an apostle **by the will of God.** God, having chosen him long before, brought His sovereign choice to realization with that most striking of conversions on the Damascus Road (Acts 9:1–9). It climaxed in his being set apart for missionary service by the Holy Spirit (Acts 13:2).

Paul, as was his custom, mentions a colaborer who was with him when he wrote: **Timothy our brother.** (Timothy is also included in the introductions to 2 Corinthians, Philippians, 1 and 2 Thessalonians, and Philemon, being noted as the companion of Paul.) Such a reference does not indicate coauthorship of those epistles. Peter is certainly clear that the epistles bearing Paul's name were written by Paul (2 Pet 3:15–16).

Paul had a unique and special confidence in and love for Timothy. Timothy had ministered to him for many years, ever since they first met on Paul's second missionary journey (Acts 19:22). Although Paul was now a prisoner, faithful Timothy was still with him. Perhaps no passage expresses Paul's feelings about his young friend more clearly than Philippians 2:19–22: "I hope in the Lord Jesus to send Timothy to you shortly, so that I also may be encouraged when I learn of your condition. For I have no one *else* of kindred spirit who will genuinely be concerned for your welfare. For they all seek after their own interests, not those of Christ Jesus. But you know of his proven worth, that he served with me in the furtherance of the gospel like a child *serving* his father."

Despite his many strengths, Timothy had a delicate constitution and was frequently sick (1 Tim 5:23). He even had an experience in Ephesus when he was timid, hesitant, perhaps ashamed and disloyal to his gift and duty, and was in need of encouragement and strength (cf. 2 Tim 1:5–14). Still, no one served Paul as faithfully in the spread of the gospel (Phil 2:22). He was Paul's true child in the faith (1 Cor 4:17). It was to Timothy that Paul wrote his final letter (2 Timothy) and passed the mantle of leadership (2 Tim 4).

Paul addresses his readers as the **saints and faithful brethren ... *who are* at Colossae. Saints and faithful brethren** are not two distinct groups; the terms are equivalent. **And** [*kai*] could be translated, "even." *Hagios,* which translates **saints,** refers to separation, in this case being separated from sin and set apart to God. **Faithful** notes the very source of that separation—saving faith. Believing saints are the only true saints. **Grace to you and peace** was the greeting Paul used to open all thirteen of his letters. Inasmuch as God is the source of both, Paul says those two blessings derive from our great God and Father.

THE GOSPEL TRUTH IS RECEIVED BY FAITH

We give thanks to God, the Father of our Lord Jesus Christ, praying always for you, since we heard of your faith in Christ Jesus ... (1:3–4*a*)

Though he admires their true and continuing saving faith, which had separated them from sin to God, Paul certainly does not begin by flattering the Colossians. He gives **thanks to God, the Father of our Lord Jesus Christ.** Paul recognizes that God is the One who is owed thanks, because salvation in all its parts is a gift from Him (Eph 2:8–9). **Always** should be considered in relation to the preceding phrase, **we give thanks to God,** not to **praying ... for you.** Paul was not always praying for the Colossians. Rather, whenever he was praying for them, he always expressed his thanks to God.

Paul is thankful to God for their faith in Christ Jesus. The Colossians are not like those who distort the gospel (Gal 1:7), or do not obey it (1 Pet 4:17). Such people will face the terrifying experience of seeing "the Lord Jesus ... revealed from heaven with His mighty angels in flaming fire, dealing out retribution to those who do not know God and to those who do not obey the gospel of our Lord Jesus. These will pay the penalty of eternal destruction, away from the presence of the Lord and from the glory of His power" (2 Thess 1:7–9). The Colossians are holy brothers in Christ, who have put faith in the Lord of the gospel.

FAITH'S DEFINITION

Pistis (**faith**) means to be persuaded that something is true and to trust in it. Far more than mere intellectual assent, it involves obedience. *Pistis* comes from the root word *peithō* ("obey"). The concept of obedience is equated with belief throughout the New Testament (cf. John 3:36; Acts 6:7; Rom 15:18; 2 Thess 1:8; Heb 5:9; 1 Pet 4:17). The Bible also speaks of the obedience of faith (Acts 6:7; Rom 1:5; 16:26).

Biblical faith is not a "leap in the dark." It is based on fact and grounded in evidence. It is defined in Hebrews 11:1 as "the assurance of *things* hoped for, the conviction of things not seen." Faith gives assurance and certainty about unseen realities.

I often have occasion to drive on roads I have never driven on before. I do not know what is around the next bend; the road could end at a cliff with a 500-foot drop. Nor do I know personally the people who built the road. However, I know enough about how highways are built to have confidence in the road. Likewise, I sometimes will eat at a restaurant I have never been to before. I trust the food is all right because I have confidence in the inspection and preparation procedures.

We trust that highways and restaurants are safe based on the evidence. And that is precisely the case with our faith in God. It is supported by convincing evidence, both from Scripture and from the testimony of those Christians who have gone before us.

Saving faith is carefully defined in Scripture and needs to be understood because there is a dead, non-saving faith that provides false security (Jas 2:14–26). True saving faith contains repentance and obedience as its elements.

Repentance is an initial element of saving faith, but it cannot be dismissed as simply another word for believing. The Greek word for "repentance" is *metanoia*, from *meta*, "after," and *noeō*, "to understand." Literally it means "afterthought" or "change of mind," but biblically its meaning does not stop there. As *metanoia* is used in the New Testament, it always speaks of a change of purpose, and specifically a turning from sin. More specifically, repentance calls for a repudiation of the old life and a turning to God for salvation (1 Thess 1:9). The repentance in saving faith involves three elements: a turning to God, a turning from evil, and an intent to serve God. No change of mind can be called true repentance without all three. Repentance is not merely being ashamed or sorry over sin, although genuine repentance always involves an element of remorse. It is a redirection of the human will, a purposeful decision to forsake all unrighteousness and pursue righteousness instead. And God has to grant it (Acts 11:18; 2 Tim 2:25). In fact, God grants the whole of saving faith: "By grace you have been saved through faith; and that not of yourselves, *it is* the gift of God; not as a result of works, so that no one may boast" (Eph 2:8–9; cf. Phil 1:29).

Although it is true that "he who believes has eternal life" (John 6:47), Jesus also said, "No one can come to Me unless the Father who sent Me draws him" (John 6:44). God effectually calls sinners to Christ and grants them the capability to exercise saving faith (cf. Matt 16:17).

The faith that God grants is permanent. In all who receive it, faith will endure. Such passages as Habakkuk 2:4, Romans 1:17, Galatians 3:11, Philippians 1:6, and Hebrews 10:38 teach that genuine saving faith can never vanish.

Like repentance, obedience is also encompassed within the bounds of saving faith. The faith that saves involves more than mere intellectual assent and emotional conviction. It also includes the resolution of the will to obey God's commands and laws.

Obedience is the hallmark of the true believer. "When a man obeys God he gives the only possible evidence that in his heart he believes God" (W. E. Vine, *An Expository Dictionary of New Testament Words*, [Old Tappan, NJ: Revell, 1966], 3:124). Such obedience will of necessity be incomplete, since the flesh ever rears its ugly head (cf. Rom 7:14–25). If not the perfection of the believer's life, however, it most certainly will be the direction.

Faith, then, must never be severed from good works. Martin Luther summed up the biblical view of the link between saving faith and good works in these words: "Good works do not make a man good, but a good man does good works" (cited in Tim Dowley, ed., *Eerdmans Handbook to the History of Christianity* [Grand Rapids: Eerdmans, 1987], 362).

FAITH'S OBJECT

Any definition of faith is also incomplete without a consideration of its object. In contrast to the contentless faith so prevalent in our culture, saving faith has as its object Christ Jesus. The relationship of faith to Jesus Christ is expressed in the New Testament by various Greek prepositions. Acts 16:31 uses the preposition *epi*, which suggests resting on a foundation. In Acts

20:21, *eis* is used, with the meaning of "to find a dwelling place in," "to go into," "to abide in," or "to find a home." Here **in** translates *en* and has the connotation of coming to a place of security and anchor. With Christ as its object, our faith is as secure as a house on a solid foundation, or a boat safely at anchor.

Charles Spurgeon illustrated the importance of faith's object by telling of two men in a boat. Caught in severe rapids, they were being swept toward a waterfall. Some men on shore tried to save them by throwing them a rope. One man caught hold of it and was pulled to safety on the shore. The other, in the panic of the moment, grabbed hold of a seemingly more substantial log that was floating by. That man was carried downstream, over the rapids, and was never seen again. Faith, represented by the rope linked to the shore, connects us to Jesus Christ and safety. Good works apart from true faith, represented in the story by the log, leads only to ruin.

THE GOSPEL TRUTH RESULTS IN LOVE

... and the love which you have for all the saints ... (1:4*b*)

Genuine faith does not exist in a vacuum but will inevitably result in a changed life. One of the visible and strong fruits of true saving faith is love for fellow believers (cf. John 13:34–35). The apostle John emphasizes that truth repeatedly in his first epistle:

> The one who says he is in the Light and *yet* hates his brother is in the darkness until now. The one who loves his brother abides in the Light and there is no cause for stumbling in him. But the one who hates his brother is in the darkness and walks in the darkness, and does not know where he is going because the darkness has blinded his eyes. (2:9–11)

> By this the children of God and the children of the devil are obvious: anyone who does not practice righteousness is not of God, nor the one who does not love his brother. (3:10)

> We know that we have passed out of death into life, because we love the brethren. He who does not love abides in death. Everyone who hates his brother is a murderer; and you know that no murderer has eternal life abiding in him. (3:14–15)

> If someone says, "I love God," and hates his brother, he is a liar; for the one who does not love his brother whom he has seen, cannot love God whom he has not seen. (4:20)

A true child of God will love fellow believers. Faith in Christ purges us of our selfishness and affinity for sinners and gives us a new attraction to the people of God. Our love for fellow Christians is a reflection of His love for us. It is also obedience to His command to "love one another, even as I have loved you" (John 13:34).

Paul gives thanks that the Colossians love all the saints. Their love was nonselective. Apparently there were no divisive cliques at Colossae, such as those that fractured the Corinthian church. Christ's love not only drew the Colossians to Himself, but also to each other.

That does not mean we are to feel the same emotional attachment toward everyone. True biblical love is so much more than an emotion; it is sacrificial service to others because they have need. We show godly love to someone when we sacrifice ourselves to meet that person's needs.

True godly love is illustrated in John 13. Verse 1 tells us that Jesus "having loved His own who were in the world, He loved them to the end." He then showed what that love meant by washing the disciples' feet (vv. 4–5). God does not expect us to feel sentimental toward each other all the time. He does expect us to serve one another (Gal 5:13).

There are two sides to the Christian life, both of which are crucial: faith and love. Genuine belief in the truth and experiential love for other believers characterizes every true believer. We are saved by faith; we are saved to love. True saving faith is more than a conviction of the mind. It transforms the heart to love.

THE GOSPEL TRUTH RESTS IN HOPE

... because of the hope laid up for you in heaven, of which you previously heard in the word of truth, the gospel ... (1:5)

Hope is one component of the great triad of Christian virtues, along with faith and love. "But now faith, hope, love, abide these three; but the greatest of these is love" (1 Cor 13:13; cf. 1 Thess 1:3; 5:8). Paul is thankful not only for the Colossians' faith and love, but also for their hope. Faith and hope are inseparably linked. We believe, and so we hope.

Paul describes that hope as laid up for you in heaven. *Apokeimai* (**laid up**) means "in store," or "reserved." Peter speaks of "an inheritance *which is* imperishable and undefiled and will not fade away, reserved in heaven for you" (1 Pet 1:4). The writer of Hebrews speaks of "[taking] hold of the hope set before us. This hope we have as an anchor of the soul, a *hope* both sure and steadfast and one which enters within the veil" (Heb 6:18–19). Hope is the Christian's anchor chain, connecting him inseparably to God's throne.

God established our hope by making us His sons. The Colossians became sons of God by believing the message they previously heard in the word of truth, the gospel. First John 3:1 says, "See how great a love the Father has bestowed upon us, that we would be called children of God." He will fulfill our hope by making us like His Son: "Beloved, now we are children of God, and it has not appeared as yet what we will be. We know that when He appears, we will be like Him, because we will see Him just as He is" (v. 2).

One result of our hope is a willingness to sacrifice the present on the altar of the future. That runs contrary to human nature. Young children, for example, have a difficult time waiting for something they want. My father warned me repeatedly while I was growing up not to sacrifice the future on the altar of the immediate. The world wants what it wants now.

The Christian has a different perspective. He is willing to forsake the present glory, comfort, and satisfaction of this present world for the future glory that is his in Christ. In contrast to the "buy now—pay later" attitude prevalent in the world, the Christian is willing to pay now and receive it later. What makes Christians willing to make such sacrifices? Hope, based on faith that the future holds something far better than the present. Paul writes in Romans 8:18, "I consider that the sufferings of this present time are not worthy to be compared with the glory that is to be revealed to us."

Moses serves as an example of one who willingly sacrificed the present because of the promise of his future hope. Hebrews 11:24–27 gives us his story: "By faith Moses, when he had grown up, refused to be called the son of Pharaoh's daughter, choosing rather to endure ill-treatment with the people of God than to enjoy the passing pleasures of sin, considering the reproach of Christ greater riches than the treasures of Egypt; for he was looking to the reward. By faith he left Egypt, not fearing the wrath of the king; for he endured, as seeing Him who is unseen."

As the adopted son of Pharaoh's daughter, Moses had access to all the wealth and power of Pharaoh's court. Yet, he turned his back on it and identified with God's suffering, poor, humbled people. Moses refused to seize the moment and enjoy the temporal pleasures of sin. He sacrificed his present prospects for a future hope. He took his stand with the oppressed Israelites, an act that led to his killing an Egyptian overseer and eventual flight from Egypt. He forfeited earthly power and glory and instead wound up herding sheep in the desert for his father-in-law to be, Jethro.

What made Moses willing to make such sacrifices? "He was looking to the reward" (Heb 11:26). Why was he willing to turn his back on the riches and power that were his in Egypt? "He endured, as seeing Him who is unseen" (Heb 11:27). Moses knew that though he suffered loss in the present, God would richly reward him in the future.

Like Moses, believers look for a hope that is in heaven. We live in the light of eternity, knowing that our citizenship is in heaven (Phil 3:20). We serve the Lord, making sacrifices here to lay up treasure in heaven. Like Paul, we set aside our prerogatives, obeying God's will and disciplining ourselves to win an incorruptible crown (cf. 2 Tim 4:8). Like Jim Elliot, missionary and martyr to the Auca Indians, we must realize that "he is no fool who gives what he cannot keep to gain what he cannot lose" (cited in Elisabeth Elliot, *Shadow of the Almighty* [San Francisco: Harper & Row, 1979], 108).

THE GOSPEL TRUTH REACHES THE WORLD

... the gospel, which has come to you, just as in all the world ... (1:6*a*)

The gospel is also universal; it **has come to you, just as in all the world.** Christianity was not just another of the local sects of the Roman Empire. It was not merely one more cult like the others at Colossae. It was and is the good news for the whole world. The gospel transcends ethnic, geographic, cultural, and political boundaries.

This universality of the gospel is repeatedly emphasized in Scripture:

> This gospel of the kingdom shall be preached in the whole world as a testimony to all the nations, and then the end will come. (Matt 24:14)

> Then Jesus again spoke to them, saying, "I am the Light of the world; he who follows Me will not walk in the darkness, but will have the Light of life." (John 8:12)

> First, I thank my God through Jesus Christ for you all, because your faith is being proclaimed throughout the whole world.... For I am not ashamed of the gospel, for it is the power of God for salvation to everyone who believes, to the Jew first and also to the Greek. (Rom 1:8, 16)

> But I say, surely they have never heard, have they? Indeed they have; "THEIR VOICE HAS GONE OUT INTO ALL THE EARTH, AND THEIR WORDS TO THE ENDS OF THE WORLD." (Rom 10:18)

> For the word of the Lord has sounded forth from you, not only in Macedonia and Achaia, but also in every place your faith toward God has gone forth, so that we have no need to say anything. (1 Thess 1:8)

> After these things I looked, and behold, a great multitude which no one could count, from every nation and *all* tribes and peoples and tongues, standing before the throne and before the Lamb, clothed in white robes, and palm branches *were* in their hands; and they cry out with a loud voice, saying, "Salvation to our God who sits on the throne, and to the Lamb." (Rev 7:9–10)

The diffusion of the gospel throughout the Roman Empire foreshadowed its spread throughout the world. It is a message of hope for all people in all cultures. The true church, the Body of Christ, is made up of people from all over the world (cf. Rev 5:9–11).

THE GOSPEL TRUTH REPRODUCES FRUIT

... it is constantly bearing fruit and increasing, even as *it has been doing* in you also since the day you heard *of it* ... (1:6*b*)

The gospel is not merely a stagnant system of ethics; it is a living, moving, and growing reality. It bears fruit and spreads. Hebrews 4:12 says, "The word of God is living and active." When the gospel enters a divinely prepared heart, it results in fruit (Matt 13:3–8). It possesses a divine energy that causes it to spread like a mustard seed growing into a tree (Matt 13:31–32). Peter says it brings spiritual growth (1 Pet 2:2).

The gospel has both an individual and a universal aspect. It is both bearing fruit and increasing. Paul tells the Colossians he is thankful the gospel had done both among them **since the day you** [the Colossians] **heard *of it*.** He is grateful they believed the gospel message when Epaphras shared it with them.

The gospel produces fruit both in the internal transformation of individuals, and also in the external growth of the church. The two concepts are interrelated. The spiritual growth of individuals will lead to new converts being won to Christ. That was the pattern of the early church. Acts 9:31 tells us that "the church throughout all Judea and Galilee and Samaria enjoyed peace, being built up ... going on in the fear of the Lord and in the comfort of the Holy Spirit," and as a result, "it continued to increase." First Thessalonians 1:6 speaks of the spiritual growth of the Thessalonians as they imitated Paul and the Lord. As a result, "the word of the Lord has sounded forth from you, not only in Macedonia and Achaia, but also in every place your faith toward God has gone forth, so that we have no need to say anything" (v. 8).

The living gospel is the power that transforms lives. As it does so, the witness of those transformed lives produces fruit, including new converts. So as the gospel produces fruit in individual lives, its influence spreads.

THE GOSPEL TRUTH IS ROOTED IN GRACE

... and understood the grace of God in truth ... (1:6*c*)

Grace is the very heart of the gospel. It is God's freely giving us the forgiveness of sin and eternal life, which we do not deserve and cannot earn. Christianity contrasts sharply with other religions, which assume man can save himself by his good works. Nothing is more clearly taught in Scripture than the truth that "by grace you have been saved through faith; and that not of yourselves, *it is* the gift of God; not as a result of works, so that no one may boast" (Eph 2:8–9).

After hearing Peter's account of the conversion of Cornelius, the rest of the apostles exclaimed, "Well then, God has granted to the Gentiles also the repentance *that leads* to life" (Acts 11:18). Lydia was saved after "the Lord opened her heart to respond to the things spoken by Paul" (Acts 16:14). Paul told the Thessalonians he was thankful "because God has chosen [them] from the beginning for salvation through sanctification by the Spirit and faith in the truth" (2 Thess 2:13). He wrote to Titus that "the grace of God has appeared, bringing salvation to all men, instructing us to deny ungodliness and worldly desires and to live sensibly, righteously and godly in the present age" (Titus 2:11–12). Salvation is a gracious act on God's part (see also Acts 15:11; 18:27; Rom 3:24; 4:1–8).

Paul describes saving grace as **the grace of God in truth.** The phrase **in truth** carries the sense of genuineness. It is truly **the grace of God** in contrast to all other claimants to the true gospel. God is freely, sovereignly merciful and forgiving. We can do nothing to cause our own salvation; God saves us freely by His grace. The hymn "Jesus Paid It All" expresses that thought in these familiar words:

For nothing good have I
Whereby Thy grace to claim.
I'll wash my garments white
In the blood of Calv'ry's Lamb.

Jesus paid it all,
All to Him I owe;
Sin had left a crimson stain,
He washed it white as snow.

THE GOSPEL TRUTH IS REPORTED BY PEOPLE

... just as you learned *it* from Epaphras, our beloved fellow bond-servant, who is a faithful servant of Christ on our behalf, and he also informed us of your love in the Spirit. (1:7–8)

Although salvation is solely by God's grace, He uses humans as channels of that grace. Jesus told the disciples in Acts 1:8 that they, in the power of the Holy Spirit, were to be His witnesses. First Corinthians 1:21 speaks of those who believed through hearing the message preached. But perhaps no passage states this truth as forcefully as Romans 10:14. "How then will they call on Him in whom they have not believed? How will they believe in Him whom they have not heard? And how will they hear without a preacher?"

As noted in the introduction, Epaphras brought the good news of God's grace to the Colossian church. They learned it from him. Paul often referred to himself as a *doulos* (**bond-servant**) of Christ (Rom 1:1; Phil 1:1; Gal 1:10; Titus 1:1). By referring to Epaphras as his **fellow bond-servant** (*sundoulos*), and calling him a faithful servant of Christ on our behalf, Paul connects Epaphras' ministry with his own. Epaphras was Paul's representative at Colossae, backed by his authority and that of the Lord Jesus. While Paul was imprisoned, unable to go to the Colossians, Epaphras ministered to them on Paul's behalf. He also informed Paul of the Colossians' **love in the Spirit,** a report that no doubt brought great joy to Paul's heart. Paul was thankful for the gospel, and for the Colossians' reception of it.

God gives us the wonderful privilege and sobering responsibility of being His agents in proclaiming the gospel of His grace. May we be faithful to share with others the gospel that has meant so much to us.

02

PAUL PRAYS FOR THE COLOSSIANS—PART 1

COLOSSIANS 1:9–11

For this reason also, since the day we heard *of it,* we have not ceased to pray for you and to ask that you may be filled with the knowledge of His will in all spiritual wisdom and understanding, so that you will walk in a manner worthy of the Lord, to please *Him* in all respects, bearing fruit in every good work and increasing in the knowledge of God; strengthened with all power, according to His glorious might, for the attaining of all steadfastness and patience ... (1:9–11)

Even without the benefit of sophisticated scientific equipment or technology, every Christian can minister directly to the spiritual well-being of other believers without seeing or speaking to them. We can play a role in their spiritual growth, and even secure God's blessings for them. The amazing means is prayer.

The ministry of an apostle consisted primarily of teaching the Word and prayer (Acts 6:4). While Paul obviously gives rich instruction to the Colossians, he also shares something of his prayers for them. Verses 9–14 are a sample of Paul's ministry of prayer on their behalf. His passionate words contain two elements: petition (vv. 9–11), and praise (vv. 12–14).

Paul acknowledged the important role the prayers of others played in his ministry: "You also joining in helping us through your prayers, so that thanks may be given by many persons on our behalf for the favor bestowed on us through *the prayers of* many" (2 Cor 1:11); "I know that this shall turn out for my deliverance through your prayers and the provision of the Spirit of Jesus Christ" (Phil 1:19); "prepare me a lodging, for I hope that through your prayers I will be given to you" (Phlm 22).

It is no surprise, then, that the New Testament exhorts us to pray for one another. We read in Ephesians 6:18, "With all prayer and petition pray at all times in the Spirit, and with this in view, be on the alert with all perseverance and petition for all the saints." Paul writes in 1 Timothy 2:1, "I urge that entreaties *and* prayers, petitions *and* thanksgivings, be made on behalf of all men." The writer of Hebrews asked of his readers, "Pray for us, for we are sure that we have a good conscience, desiring to conduct ourselves honorably in all things" (13:18).

The Bible is replete with examples of God's people praying for each other:

- Job prayed for his friends (Job 42:10).
- Moses prayed for Aaron (Deut 9:20) and Miriam (Num 12:13).
- Samuel prayed for Israel (1 Sam 7:5, 9).
- David prayed for Israel (2 Sam 24:17) and Solomon (1 Chr 29:18–19).
- Hezekiah prayed for Judah (2 Kgs 19:14–19).
- Isaiah prayed for the people of God (Isa 63:15–64:12).
- Daniel prayed for Israel (Dan 9:3–19).

- Ezekiel prayed for Israel (Ezek 9:8).
- Nehemiah prayed for Judah (Neh 1:4–11).
- Jesus prayed for His disciples (John 17:9–24).
- The Jerusalem church prayed for Peter's release from prison (Acts 12:5).
- Paul prayed for Christians (e.g., Rom 1:9–10; Eph 1:16–19).
- Epaphras prayed for the Colossians (Col 4:12).

Because prayer is so important, Paul starts his letter by sharing the nature of his prayers for the Colossians before he begins to teach them. Two elements compose the content of his prayer: petition (vv. 9–11) and praise (vv. 12–14).

THE PETITION

For this reason also, since the day we heard *of it,* we have not ceased to pray for you and to ask that you may be filled with the knowledge of His will in all spiritual wisdom and understanding … (1:9)

For this reason refers to the favorable report Paul had received from Epaphras (v. 8). Since the day Paul heard that report, he had been praying for the Colossians. It may seem unnecessary to pray for those who are doing well. Much of our prayer time focuses on those who are struggling, facing difficulties, or fallen into sin or physical distress. Paul, however, knew that the knowledge that others are progressing in the faith should never lead us to stop praying for them. Rather, it should encourage prayer for their greater progress. The enemy may reserve his strongest opposition for those who have the most potential for expanding God's cause in the world.

Such unceasing or recurring prayer (1 Thess 5:17) demands first of all an attitude of God-consciousness. That does not mean to be constantly in the act of verbal prayer, but to view everything in life in relation to God. For example, if we meet someone, we immediately consider where they stand with God. If we hear of something bad happening, we react by praying for God to act in the situation because we know He cares. If we hear of something good that has happened, we respond with immediate praise to God for it because we know He is glorified. When Paul looked around his world, everything he saw prompted him to prayer in some way. When he thought of or heard about one of his beloved churches, it moved him toward communion with God.

Nehemiah is an example of one who prayed without ceasing. After King Artaxerxes demanded the reason for his sadness, Nehemiah told him of the destruction of Jerusalem. Asked by the king for his request, he prayed a quick, brief prayer before replying (Neh 2:4). In the midst of a stressful situation, Nehemiah was conscious of God's character and purposes.

A second aspect of unceasing prayer is people-consciousness. We cannot effectively pray for people unless we are aware of their needs. Paul exhorted the Colossians to keep alert in prayer (4:2), while to the Ephesians he wrote, "With all prayer and petition pray at all times in the Spirit, and with this in view, be on the alert with all perseverance and petition for all the saints" (Eph 6:18).

The two elements of praying without ceasing came together in Paul's prayer life. His love for God led him to seek unbroken communion with Him. His love for people drove him to unceasing prayer on their behalf. The prayers of Paul recorded in his letters are a precious legacy. They reveal his heart and are models for us to emulate. This text records the first of those prayers.

Paul's petition is that the Colossians **be filled with the knowledge of His will.** *Plēroō* (**filled**) means to be completely filled, or totally controlled. The disciples' hearts were filled with sorrow when Jesus told them of His departure (John 16:6). Luke 5:26 tells us the crowd was filled with fear after Jesus healed the paralytic. The scribes and Pharisees were filled with rage after Jesus healed on the Sabbath (Luke 6:11). The disciples were filled with the Holy Spirit (Acts 4:31), while Stephen was full of faith (Acts 6:5). In each case they were totally under the control of what filled them.

Paul wants the Colossians to be totally controlled by **knowledge.** *Epignōsis* (**knowledge**) consists of the normal Greek word for *knowledge* (*gnōsis*) with an added preposition (*epi*), which intensifies the meaning. The knowledge Paul wants the Colossians to have is a deep and thorough knowledge.

Knowledge is a central theme in Paul's writings. He said of the Corinthians, "In everything you were enriched in Him, in all speech and all knowledge" (1 Cor 1:5). He prayed that "the God of our Lord Jesus Christ, the Father of glory" would give the Ephesians "a spirit of wisdom and of revelation in the knowledge of Him" (Eph 1:17). To the Philippians he wrote, "This I pray, that your love may abound still more and more in real knowledge and all discernment" (Phil 1:9). In Colossians 2:3 we learn that all the treasures of wisdom and knowledge are hidden in Christ. Our new self "is being renewed to a true knowledge" (Col 3:10). As those verses indicate, true biblical knowledge is not speculative but issues in obedience.

The denial of absolutes, particularly in the area of morals, characterizes our society. Without a source of authority to provide absolute standards, virtually anything goes. What moral values are enforced are often arbitrary, based merely on human opinion. But for the Christian the authoritative Word of God provides absolutes. Those absolutes are the basis upon which all truth about God and all standards of faith and conduct are set. Because knowledge of those absolutes is the basis for correct behavior and ultimate judgment, it is crucial that Christians know God's revealed truth. Ignorance is not bliss, nor can anyone please God on the basis of principles they do not know.

So the Bible views knowledge of doctrinal absolutes as foundational to godly living. Most of Paul's letters begin by laying a doctrinal foundation before giving practical exhortations. For example, Paul gives eleven chapters of doctrine in Romans before turning to godly living in chapter 12. Galatians 1–4 are doctrinal, chapters 5 and 6 practical. The first three chapters of Ephesians detail our position in Christ, while the last three urge us to live accordingly. Philippians and Colossians also conform to the same pattern of doctrine preceding practical exhortations. Godly living is directly linked in Scripture to knowledge of doctrinal truth.

The Bible warns of the danger of a lack of knowledge. Proverbs 19:2 says that "it is not good for a person to be without knowledge." It was for lack of knowledge that Israel went into exile (Isa 5:13), and God says in Hosea 4:6, "My people are destroyed for lack of knowledge." First Corinthians 14:20 warns us, "Do not be children in your thinking; yet in evil be infants, but in your thinking be mature." Ephesians 4:13–14 tells us that lack of knowledge produces "children, tossed here and there by waves and carried about by every wind of doctrine, by the trickery of men, by craftiness in deceitful scheming." Verse 18 describes unbelievers as "being darkened in their understanding, excluded from the life of God because of the ignorance that is in them."

How does a person obtain knowledge? First, he must desire it. In John 7:17 Jesus says, "If anyone is willing to do His will, he will know of the teaching, whether it is of God or *whether* I speak from Myself." That thought is echoed in Hosea 6:3, "Let us know, let us press on to know the LORD." Second, he must depend on the Holy Spirit. It is through Him that we know the things God has revealed to us (cf. 1 Cor 2:10–12). Finally, he must study the Scriptures, for they make the believer "adequate, equipped for every good work" (2 Tim 3:16–17). Perhaps the most graphic text related to the pursuit of divine truth is Job 28.

Paul prays that the knowledge we have would be of His will. God's will is not a secret; He has revealed it in His Word. For example, it is God's desire that a person be saved (1 Tim 2:4; 2 Pet 3:9). Once a person is saved, it is God's will that he be filled with the Spirit. Ephesians 5:17–18 says, "Do not be foolish, but understand what the will of the Lord is. And do not get drunk with wine, for that is dissipation, but be filled with the Spirit." Furthermore, sanctification is God's will: "For this is the will of God, your sanctification" (1 Thess 4:3). God also wills that the believer be submissive to the government. Peter writes, "Submit yourselves for the Lord's sake to every human institution ... for such is the will of God" (1 Pet 2:13, 15). Suffering may also be God's will for the believer: "Those also who suffer according to the will of God shall entrust their souls to a faithful Creator in doing what is right" (1 Pet 4:19). Finally, giving thanks is God's will. Paul writes, "In everything give thanks; for this is God's will for you in Christ Jesus" (1 Thess 5:18).

Having the knowledge of God's Word control our minds is the key to righteous living. What controls your thoughts will control your behavior. Self-control is a result of mind-control, which is dependent on knowledge. Knowledge of God's Word will lead to **all spiritual wisdom and understanding.** Though the terms **wisdom** and **understanding** may be synonymous, *sophia* (**wisdom**) may be the broader of the two terms. It refers to the ability to collect and concisely organize principles from Scripture. *Sunesis* (**understanding**) could be a more specialized term, referring to the application of those principles to everyday life. Both *sophia* and *sunesis* are spiritual; they deal in the nonphysical realm and have the Holy Spirit as their source.

Believing, submissive Bible study leads to the knowledge of God's will. A mind saturated with such knowledge will also be able to comprehend general principles of godly behavior. With that wisdom will come understanding of how to apply those principles to the situations of life. That progression will inevitably result in godly character and practice.

THE RESULTS

... so that you will walk in a manner worthy of the Lord, to please *Him* in all respects, bearing fruit in every good work and increasing in the knowledge of God; strengthened with all power, according to His glorious might, for the attaining of all steadfastness and patience; joyously ... (1:10–11)

In verses 10–11, Paul lists five purposes that are fulfilled in such spiritual knowledge.

A WORTHY WALK

... so that you will walk in a manner worthy of the Lord, to please *Him* in all respects ... (1:10*a*)

Walk is used in the Bible to refer to one's pattern of daily conduct. A mind controlled by knowledge, wisdom, and understanding produces a life **worthy of the Lord.** Although it seems impossible that anyone could walk worthy of the Lord, that is the teaching of Scripture. Paul desired the Thessalonians to "walk in a manner worthy of the God who calls you into His own kingdom and glory" (1 Thess 2:12). He exhorted the

Ephesians to "walk in a manner worthy of the calling with which you have been called" (Eph 4:1). He told the Philippians to "conduct yourselves in a manner worthy of the gospel of Christ" (Phil 1:27).

God has not left us to our own resources for walking the worthy walk. Paul wrote to the Galatians, "I have been crucified with Christ; and it is no longer I who live, but Christ lives in me; and the *life* which I now live in the flesh I live by faith in the Son of God, who loved me and gave Himself up for me" (Gal 2:20). Christ dwells in us in the person of the Holy Spirit. Paul prayed for the Ephesians "that He would grant you, according to the riches of His glory, to be strengthened with power through His Spirit in the inner man, so that Christ may dwell in your hearts through faith" (Eph 3:16–17). Trying to walk worthy in our own strength is doomed to failure. Martin Luther stated that truth clearly in his hymn "A Mighty Fortress is Our God":

> Did we in our own strength confide
> Our striving would be losing,
> Were not the right Man on our side,
> The Man of God's own choosing.
> Dost ask who that may be?
> Christ Jesus, it is He.
> Lord Sabaoth His name,
> From age to age the same.
> And He must win the battle.

The New Testament describes several features of the worthy walk. We are to walk in humility (Eph 4:1–3); in purity (Rom 13:13, LSB); in contentedness (1 Cor 7:17); by faith (2 Cor 5:7); in good works (Eph 2:10); different from the world (Eph 4:17–32); in love (Eph 5:2); in light (Eph 5:8); in wisdom (Eph 5:15); and in truth (3 John 3–4). Such a walk will please Him in all respects.

A FRUITFUL LIFE

... bearing fruit in every good work ... (1:10*b*)

Fruitfullness also results from knowledge. Fruit is the by-product of righteousness. It is the mark of every redeemed individual. Jesus said in John 15:8, "My Father is glorified by this, that you bear much fruit, and *so* prove to be My disciples" (cf. vv. 2, 5–6). Paul told the Romans, "You also were made to die to the Law through the body of Christ, so that you might be joined to another, to Him who was raised from the dead, in order that we might bear fruit for God" (Rom 7:4).

The Bible defines **fruit** in various ways. Here Paul speaks of **bearing fruit in every good work.** Converts are referred to as fruit. Paul spoke of the household of Stephanas as the "first fruits of Achaia" (1 Cor 16:15). He also desired some fruit among the Romans (Rom 1:13). Hebrews 13:15 defines praise as fruit: "Through Him then, let us continually offer up a sacrifice of praise to God, that is, the fruit of lips that give thanks to His name." Giving money can also be fruit (Rom 15:26–28). Godly living is fruit, as indicated when the writer of Hebrews tells us that God's discipline produces in us "the peaceful fruit of righteousness" (Heb 12:11). Finally, the holy attitudes mentioned in Galatians 5:22–23 are referred to as "the fruit of the Spirit."

What produces fruit in believers' lives? First, union with Christ. Jesus said in John 15:4–5, "Abide in Me, and I in you. As the branch cannot bear fruit of itself unless it abides in the vine, so neither *can* you unless you abide in Me. I am the vine, you are the branches; he who abides in Me and I in him, he bears much fruit, for apart from Me you can do nothing."

Second, wisdom is a necessary prerequisite for bearing fruit. "But the wisdom from above is first pure, then peaceable, gentle, reasonable, full of mercy and good fruits, unwavering, without hypocrisy" (Jas 3:17). Lack of fruit is directly related to lack of spiritual wisdom. Finally, diligent effort on the Christian's part is required, as Peter writes:

> Applying all diligence, in your faith supply moral excellence, and in *your* moral excellence, knowledge, and in *your* knowledge, self-control, and in *your* self-control, perseverance, and in *your* perseverance, godliness, and in *your* godliness, brotherly kindness, and in *your* brotherly kindness, love. For

> if these *qualities* are yours and are increasing, they render you neither useless nor unfruitful in the true knowledge of our Lord Jesus Christ. (2 Pet 1:5–8)

GROWTH

... increasing in the knowledge of God ... (1:10*c*)

A third result of knowledge is spiritual growth. Spiritual growth is progressing **in the knowledge of God.** *Tē epignōsei* (**in the knowledge**) is an instrumental dative case. It indicates the means by which our **increasing,** or growth, takes place. The knowledge of God revealed in His Word is crucial to spiritual growth. Peter wrote, "Like newborn babies, long for the pure milk of the word, so that by it you may grow in respect to salvation" (1 Pet 2:2). As always, the Holy Spirit infuses our own efforts with God's enabling grace (2 Pet 3:18), without which we could not grow.

The marks of spiritual growth include: first, a deeper love for God's Word. "O how I love Your law! It is my meditation all the day" (Ps 119:97).

Second, spiritual growth is reflected in a more perfect obedience.

> By this we know that we have come to know Him, if we keep His commandments. The one who says, "I have come to know Him," and does not keep His commandments, is a liar, and the truth is not in him; but whoever keeps His word, in him the love of God has truly been perfected. (1 John 2:3–5)

Third, spiritual growth will result in an enlarged faith. "We ought always to give thanks to God for you, brethren, as is *only* fitting, because your faith is greatly enlarged" (2 Thess 1:3; cf. 2 Cor 10:15).

A fourth mark of spiritual growth is a greater love: "This I pray, that your love may abound still more and more in real knowledge and all discernment" (Phil 1:9).

STRENGTH

... strengthened with all power, according to His glorious might ... (1:11*a*)

A fourth result of knowledge is spiritual strength. *Dunamoumenoi* (**strengthened**) is a present participle, signifying continuous action. God is not like a booster rocket giving believers an initial boost of power and then leaving them to fly on their own. Believers are continually **strengthened with all power** throughout their Christian lives.

The measure of that power is **according to His glorious might. Glorious** is from *doxa* and refers to the manifestation of God's attributes. **Might** translates *kratos,* which refers to strength in action. It refers to God eleven out of the twelve times it is used in the New Testament. The **power** available to us is the limitless power of God Himself.

God's power is manifested in us through the ministry of the Holy Spirit. Our Lord told the disciples they would receive power after the Holy Spirit came upon them (Acts 1:8). Paul prayed for the Ephesians that they would be "strengthened with power through His Spirit in the inner man" (Eph 3:16). To the Romans he wrote, "May the God of hope fill you with all joy and peace in believing, so that you will abound in hope by the power of the Holy Spirit" (Rom 15:13). That power is available to the believer who is filled with the knowledge of God's Word.

ENDURANCE

... for the attaining of all steadfastness and patience; joyously ... (1:11*b*)

Paul gives one last result of true spiritual knowledge: joyous endurance of trials. Knowledge of God's promises and purposes revealed in Scripture gives the strength to endure trials and suffering. *Hupomonē* (**steadfastness**) and *makrothumia* (**patience**) are closely related. If there is a distinction, it is that *hupomonē* refers to being patient in circumstances, whereas *makrothumia* refers to patience with people (Richard C. Trench, *Synonyms of the New Testament* [Grand Rapids: Eerdmans, 1983], 198). Both refer to the patient enduring of trials.

Paul does not have in mind a stoic, teeth-gritting endurance. The strength provided by knowledge of God's Word allows the believer to endure trials **joyously,** literally "with joy" (*meta charis*). Commentators are divided on whether *meta charis* should be connected with **steadfastness** and **patience** in verse 11, or with **giving thanks** in verse 12. It seems best, however, to connect the phrase with verse 11. **Giving thanks** (v. 12) already includes the element of joy. Knowledge of God's truth gives us the ability to endure trials joyously, as did Paul himself (cf. Acts 16:25).

It was Paul's constant prayer for the Colossians that they be filled with the knowledge of God's will. He knew that only when believers are controlled by that knowledge can they walk worthy of the Lord and please Him. Paul knew further that such knowledge was required for a fruitful life, spiritual growth, strength, and joyful endurance of trials.

03

PAUL PRAYS FOR THE COLOSSIANS—PART 2

COLOSSIANS 1:12–14

Giving thanks to the Father, who has qualified us to share in the inheritance of the saints in Light.

For He rescued us from the domain of darkness, and transferred us to the kingdom of His beloved Son, in whom we have redemption, the forgiveness of sins. (1:12–14)

Paul's prayer is a model or pattern for all believers to follow. Like his prayers here and elsewhere, our prayers should include praise as well as petitions. To the Philippians Paul wrote, "Be anxious for nothing, but in everything by prayer and supplication with thanksgiving let your requests be made known to God" (Phil 4:6). In 1 Timothy 2:1 he urged that "entreaties *and* prayers, petitions *and* thanksgivings, be made on behalf of all men." Later he told the Colossians to "yourselves to prayer, keeping alert in it with *an attitude of* thanksgiving" (Col 4:2). Paul constantly gave thanks in his prayers (cf. Acts 27:35; Rom 1:8; 1 Tim 1:12).

Giving thanks is too often demoted to a secondary place in the prayers of Christ's people. Our attitude in approaching God is often reminiscent of the leech's daughters: "Give, Give" (Prov 30:15). We are quick to make our requests and slow to thank God for His answers. Because God so often answers our prayers, we come to expect it. We forget that it is only by His grace that we receive anything from Him.

The Bible repeatedly stresses the importance of giving thanks. "Offer to God a sacrifice of thanksgiving" (Ps 50:14). "Let them give thanks to the LORD for His lovingkindness, and for His wonders to the sons of men! Let them also offer sacrifices of thanksgiving, and tell of His works with joyful singing" (Ps 107:21–22). "It is good to give thanks to the LORD, and to sing praises to Your name, O Most High" (Ps 92:1). "Always giving thanks for all things in the name of our Lord Jesus Christ to God, even the Father" (Eph 5:20). "Whatever you do in word or deed, *do* all in the name of the Lord Jesus, giving thanks through Him to God the Father" (Col 3:17). "Through Him then, let us continually offer up a sacrifice of praise to God, that is, the fruit of lips that give thanks to His name" (Heb 13:15). Thanksgiving should permeate our speech, our songs, and our prayers.

Our Lord knew the importance of giving thanks. In Matthew 11:25 He said, "I praise You, Father, Lord of heaven and earth, that You have hidden these things from *the* wise and intelligent and have revealed them to infants." Before feeding the five thousand, Jesus "took the loaves, and having given thanks, He distributed to those who were seated" (John 6:11). Just before raising Lazarus from the dead, "Jesus raised His eyes, and said, 'Father, I thank You that You have heard Me'" (John 11:41).

Revelation 7:11–12 tells us that the angels give thanks: "All the angels were standing around the throne and *around* the elders and the four living creatures; and they fell on their faces before the throne and worshiped God, saying, 'Amen, blessing and glory and wisdom and thanksgiving and honor and power and might, *be* to our God forever and ever. Amen.'"

David (2 Sam 22:50; Ps 28:7), the Levites (1 Chr 16:4; Neh 12:24), Asaph and his relatives (1 Chr 16:7), Daniel (Dan 6:10), and the priests, Levites, and descendants of Asaph (Ezra 3:10–11) also gave thanks to God.

In addition to those positive examples, the Bible teaches that failing to give thanks characterizes the wicked. One indictment of unbelievers is that "even though they knew God, they did not honor Him as God or give thanks" (Rom 1:21). Evil men are marked by ungratefullness (Luke 6:35; 2 Tim 3:2).

Scripture instructs us to thank God for many things. We are to thank Him for who He is. Psalm 30:4 says, "Sing praise to the LORD, you His godly ones, and give thanks to His holy name" (cf. Ps 97:12). We should also thank God for His nearness. "We give thanks to You, O God, we give thanks, for Your name is near" (Ps 75:1). Paul gave thanks to God for his salvation and his opportunity to serve Him: "I thank Christ Jesus our Lord, who has strengthened me, because He considered me faithful, putting me into service, even though I was formerly a blasphemer and a persecutor and a violent aggressor. Yet I was shown mercy because I acted ignorantly in unbelief" (1 Tim 1:12–13).

The apostle also gave thanks for the spiritual growth of others: "We ought always to give thanks to God for you, brethren, as is *only* fitting, because your faith is greatly enlarged, and the love of each one of you toward one another grows *ever* greater" (2 Thess 1:3).

Even mundane things like food call for giving thanks (1 Tim 4:3–4). First Thessalonians 5:18 sums it up: "In everything give thanks; for this is God's will for you in Christ Jesus."

What makes Christians most thankful is the work of Christ. In 2 Corinthians 9:15, Paul exclaims, "Thanks be to God for His indescribable gift!" He gave thanks for the result of the work of Christ, which is our salvation (cf. 1 Cor 1:4). That is also his theme in Colossians 1:12–14. Paul sums up the doctrine of salvation in three great truths: inheritance, deliverance, and transference. They are both a description of salvation and a cause for thanksgiving. He unfolds the specifics of his gratitude in those verses.

INHERITANCE

... giving thanks to the Father, who has qualified us to share in the inheritance of the saints in Light. (1:12)

Father emphasizes the personal, relational aspect of our union with God. Before our salvation, God was our Judge. We stood condemned before Him for violating His holy, just laws. But when, through the grace of God, we placed our faith in Christ, God ceased being our sentencing Judge and became our gracious Father.

Not only has God adopted us as His sons, but He has also **qualified us to share in the inheritance of the saints in Light. Qualified** is from *hikanoō*, a word used only here and in 2 Corinthians 3:6 in the New Testament. It means "to make sufficient, to empower, to authorize, to make fit." We are not qualified through our own efforts. God has qualified us through the finished work of Christ.

Before God saved us by His grace we were truly unqualified for our inheritance. Several passages in Ephesians describe our helpless condition:

> You were dead in your trespasses and sins, in which you formerly walked according to the course of this world, according to the prince of the power of the air, of the spirit

> that is now working in the sons of disobedience. Among them we too all formerly lived in the lusts of our flesh, indulging the desires of the flesh and of the mind, and were by nature children of wrath, even as the rest. (2:1–3)

> *Remember* that you were at that time separate from Christ, excluded from the commonwealth of Israel, and strangers to the covenants of promise, having no hope and without God in the world. (2:12)

> This I say, and affirm together with the Lord, that you walk no longer just as the Gentiles also walk, in the futility of their mind, being darkened in their understanding, excluded from the life of God because of the ignorance that is in them, because of the hardness of their heart; and they, having become callous, have given themselves over to sensuality for the practice of every kind of impurity with greediness. (4:17–19)

Before our salvation, we were dominated by the evil world system; its wicked ruler, Satan; and our own fallen, sinful, human natures. We were Christless, stateless, covenantless, hopeless, godless. Our minds were given to futility; our understanding was darkened. We were cut off from the life of God, ignorant, hardhearted, callous, immoral, impure, and greedy. The only thing we were qualified to receive from God was His wrath. And that is what we would have received, if not for God's mercy toward us.

God has by grace **qualified** the unqualified to share in the inheritance. The Greek text literally reads, "for the portion of the lot" (*eis tēn merida tou klērou*). The partitive genitive (*tou klērou*) means that we each receive our own individual allotment or portion of the total inheritance. Paul here alludes to the partitioning of Israel's inheritance in Canaan (cf. Num 26:52–56; 33:51–54; Josh 14:1–2). Just as the Israelites received their inheritance in the Promised Land, so also do we receive our portion of the divine inheritance.

The Bible has much to say about our **inheritance.** It consists first of eternal life. Jesus said in Matthew 19:29, "Everyone who has left houses or brothers or sisters or father or mother or children or farms for My name's sake, will receive many times as much, and will inherit eternal life." Eternal life is far more than endless existence. It is a quality of life; Christ's life lived in the believer (Gal 2:20; cf. 1 John 5:20). Second, our inheritance includes the earth. In the Sermon on the Mount, our Lord said that believers would inherit the earth (Matt 5:5). That focuses on the future aspect of our inheritance, when we will rule with Christ in the millennial kingdom (Rev 20:6). The knowledge that we will inherit the restored earth should free us from the present pursuit of material possessions. Someday we will receive far more than we could ever gain in this life. Third, we inherit all the promises of God. The writer of Hebrews exhorts us to be "imitators of those who through faith and patience inherit the promises" (Heb 6:12).

When do we receive our inheritance? The present tense participle *hikanōsanti* (**qualified**) indicates we have it now (cf. Eph 1:11). We have already been transferred from the domain of darkness into Christ's kingdom (Col 1:13). We are already fellow heirs with Christ (Rom 8:16–17). The full possession of that inheritance, however, is yet future. Peter refers to it as "an inheritance *which is* imperishable and undefiled and will not fade away, reserved in heaven for you" (1 Pet 1:4). It will be ours forever. Hebrews 9:15 depicts it as an eternal inheritance.

Paul further defines our inheritance as that of **the saints in Light.** *Hagiōn* (**saints**) refers to those who have been separated from the world and set apart to God. The inheritance belongs to that group alone. First Corinthians 6:9–10 asks the rhetorical question, "Do you not know that the unrighteous will not inherit the kingdom of God? Do not be deceived; neither fornicators, nor idolaters, nor adulterers, nor effeminate, nor homosexuals, nor thieves, nor *the* covetous, nor drunkards, nor revilers, nor swindlers, will inherit the kingdom of God."

Ephesians 5:5 echoes that thought: "For this you know with certainty, that no immoral or impure person or covetous man, who is an idolater, has an inheritance in the kingdom of Christ and God." And Galatians 5:21 adds that "those who practice such things will not inherit the kingdom of God."

The saints' inheritance is **in Light.** Light represents two things biblically. Intellectually, it represents truth (Ps 119:130). Morally, it represents purity (Eph 5:8–14). In contrast to Israel's earthly inheritance, the saints' inheritance is in the light—the spiritual realm of truth and purity where God Himself dwells (1 Tim 6:16). In his defense before King Agrippa in Acts 26, Paul spoke of the Lord's commissioning him to preach to the Gentiles. The Lord told Paul that He was sending him "to open their eyes so that they may turn from darkness to light and from the dominion of Satan to God, that they may receive forgiveness of sins and an inheritance among those who have been sanctified by faith in Me" (v. 18). Paul no doubt had that event in mind when he wrote Colossians 1:12–14. The saints are those who have turned from sinful darkness to righteous light (cf. Eph 5:8; 1 John 1:7).

God has graciously given us a guarantee for our inheritance. That guarantee is the indwelling Holy Spirit. In Ephesians 1:13–14, Paul writes, "You were sealed in Him with the Holy Spirit of promise, who is given as a pledge of our inheritance." "Pledge" translates *arrabōn,* which is similar to the modern Greek word for engagement ring. *Arrabōn* could also be translated "guarantee," or "down-payment." God has given us the Holy Spirit as the first installment on our future inheritance. That is an objective fact, not dependent on our feelings. Studying "the word of His grace, which is able to build *you* up and to give *you* the inheritance among all those who are sanctified" (Acts 20:32) results in a greater richness and understanding of our glorious inheritance.

So He has given us the Spirit and the Word to give us confidence and understanding of that inheritance. No wonder Paul prayed that "the eyes of your heart may be enlightened, so that you will know what is the hope of His calling, what are the riches of the glory of His inheritance in the saints" (Eph 1:18).

DELIVERANCE

For He rescued us from the domain of darkness ... (1:13*a*)

A second cause for thanksgiving is our spiritual liberation. **Rescued** is from *ruomai,* which means "to draw to oneself," or "to deliver." God drew us out of Satan's kingdom to Himself. That event was the new birth. We are not gradually, progressively delivered from Satan's power. When we placed our faith in Christ, we were instantly delivered. "Therefore if anyone is in Christ, *he is* a new creature; the old things passed away; behold, new things have come" (2 Cor 5:17). Believers do not need deliverance from the dominion of sin and Satan; they need to act as those who have been delivered (cf. Rom 6:2, 7, 11).

Those who receive the Lord Jesus Christ have been rescued from **the domain of darkness.** *Exousias* (**domain**) could be translated "power," "jurisdiction," or "authority." Our Lord used the phrase **domain of darkness** (*exousias tou skotous*) to refer to the supernatural forces of Satan marshalled against Him at His arrest (Luke 22:53). The triumph of the domain of darkness was short-lived, however. A few hours later, Jesus forever shattered Satan's power by His death on the cross. You need not fear that power, for "greater is He who is in you than he who is in the world" (1 John 4:4). Through His death, Jesus crushed Satan and delivered us from his dark kingdom.

TRANSFERENCE

... and transferred us to the kingdom of His beloved Son, in whom we have redemption, the forgiveness of sins. (1:13*b*, 14)

Paul continues the litany of blessings that draw out his gratitude by describing our new domain. *Methistēmi* (**transferred**) means to remove or change. It is used in Acts 13:22 to speak of God's removing Saul from being king. It was used in the ancient world to speak of the displacement of a conquered people to another land. The verb speaks here of our total removal from the domain of satanic darkness to the glorious light of the kingdom of Christ.

Kingdom refers to more than the future millennial kingdom, when Jesus will reign on earth for a thousand years. Nor does it speak merely of the general rule of God over His creation. The kingdom is a spiritual reality right now. Paul gives us a definition of it in Romans 14:17: "The kingdom of God is not eating and drinking, but righteousness and peace and joy in the Holy Spirit." The kingdom is the special relationship men in this age have with God through Jesus Christ. A kingdom in its most basic sense is a group of people ruled by a king. Christians have acknowledged Christ as their King and are subjects in His kingdom. They have been **transferred ... to the kingdom of His beloved Son.** The Greek text literally reads, "the Son of His love" (*tou huiou tēs agapēs autou*). The Father gives the kingdom to the Son He loves, then to everyone who loves the Son (Luke 12:32).

Although Christ does not yet rule on earth, He is no less a king. In response to Pilate's question, "Are You the King of the Jews?" Jesus replied, "*It is as* you say" (Matt 27:11). He reigns in eternity, rules now over His church, and one day will return to rule the earth as King of kings.

There is a tremendous responsibility that accompanies being part of Christ's kingdom. As subjects of that kingdom, we must properly represent the King. Paul admonished the Thessalonians to "walk in a manner worthy of the God who calls you into His own kingdom and glory" (1 Thess 2:12). Even their persecution was a plain indication of God's righteous judgment so they might be considered worthy of the kingdom of God, for which indeed they were suffering (2 Thess 1:5). The writer of Hebrews reminds us, "Since we receive a kingdom which cannot be shaken, let us show gratitude, by which we may offer to God an acceptable service with reverence and awe" (Heb 12:28).

Before we could be fit subjects for Christ's kingdom we needed **redemption, the forgiveness of sins.** *Apolutrōsis* (**redemption**) is one of the magnificent New Testament words expressing a blessed aspect of the work of Christ on our behalf. Alongside such terms as *sacrifice, offering, propitiation, ransom, justification, adoption,* and *reconciliation,* **redemption** attempts to describe the riches of our salvation. It means "to deliver by payment of a ransom," and was used to speak of freeing slaves from bondage. The meaning of *apolutrōsis* is expressed in our English word *emancipation.* The Septuagint uses a related word to speak of Israel's deliverance from bondage in Egypt. *Apolutrōsis* is used in several places in the New Testament to speak of Christ's freeing us from slavery to sin. In Ephesians 1:7, Paul writes, "In Him we have redemption through

His blood, the forgiveness of our trespasses, according to the riches of His grace." To the Corinthians he wrote, "By His doing you are in Christ Jesus, who became to us wisdom from God, and righteousness and sanctification, and redemption" (1 Cor 1:30). In the midst of perhaps the most thorough soteriological passage in the New Testament, Paul writes that we are "justified as a gift by His grace through the redemption which is in Christ Jesus" (Rom 3:24).

Redemption results in **the forgiveness of sins.** *Aphesin* (**forgiveness**) refers to pardon, or remission of penalty. It is a composite of two Greek words, *apo*, "from," and *hiēmi*, "to send." Because Christ redeemed us, God has sent away our sins; they will never be found again. "As far as the east is from the west, so far has He removed our transgressions from us" (Ps 103:12). "He will again have compassion on us; He will tread our iniquities under foot. Yes, You will cast all their sins into the depths of the sea" (Mic 7:19).

So Christ's death on our behalf paid the price to redeem us. On that basis, God forgave our sins, granted us an inheritance, delivered us from the power of darkness, and made us subjects of Christ's kingdom. Those wonderful truths should cause us to give thanks to God continually, as did Paul in his prayer. And when we contemplate all He has done for us, how can we do any less than pray to be filled with the knowledge of His will?

04

THE PREEMINENCE OF JESUS CHRIST

COLOSSIANS 1:15–19

He is the image of the invisible God, the firstborn of all creation. For by Him all things were created, *both* in the heavens and on earth, visible and invisible, whether thrones or dominions or rulers or authorities—all things have been created through Him and for Him. He is before all things, and in Him all things hold together. He is also head of the body, the church; and He is the beginning, the firstborn from the dead, so that He Himself will come to have first place in everything. For it was the *Father's* good pleasure for all the fullness to dwell in Him ... (1:15–19)

The Bible is supremely the book about the Lord Jesus Christ. The Old Testament records the preparation for His coming. The gospels present Him as God in human flesh, come into the world to save sinners. In Acts, the message of salvation in Christ begins to be spread throughout the world. The epistles detail the theology of Christ's work and personification of Christ in His Body, the church. Finally, Revelation presents Christ on the throne, reigning as King of kings and Lord of lords.

Every part of Scripture testifies about Jesus Christ. Luke 24:27 says, "Beginning with Moses and with all the prophets, [Jesus] explained to them the things concerning Himself in all the Scriptures." In John 5:39, Jesus said of the Scriptures, "It is these that testify about Me." Philip preached Christ to the Ethiopian eunuch by using the book of Isaiah (Acts 8:35).

But of all the Bible's teaching about Jesus Christ, none is more significant than Colossians 1:15–19. This dramatic and powerful passage removes any needless doubt or confusion over Jesus' true identity. It is vital to a proper understanding of the Christian faith.

As mentioned in the introduction, much of the heresy threatening the Colossian church centered on the Person of Christ. The heretics, denying His humanity, viewed Christ as one of many lesser descending spirit beings that emanated from God. They taught a form of philosophic dualism, postulating that spirit was good and matter was evil. Hence, a good emanation like Christ could never take on a body composed of evil matter. The idea that God Himself could become man was absurd to them. Thus, they also denied His deity.

Nor was Christ adequate for salvation, according to the errorists. Salvation required a superior, mystical, secret knowledge, beyond that of the gospel of Christ. It also involved worshiping the good emanations (angels) and keeping the Jewish ceremonial laws.

In the first three chapters of Colossians, Paul confronts the Colossian heresy head on. He rejects their denial of Christ's humanity, pointing out that it is in Him that "all the fullness of Deity dwells in bodily form" (2:9). Paul also rejects their worship of angels (2:18), and their ceremonialism (2:16–17). He emphatically denies that any secret knowledge is required for salvation, pointing out that in Christ "are hidden all the treasures of wisdom and knowledge" (2:3; cf. 1:27; 3:1–4).

By far the most serious aspect of the Colossian heresy was its rejection of Christ's deity. Before getting to the other issues, Paul makes an emphatic defense of that crucial doctrine. Christians would do well to follow his example in their confrontations with cultists. The primary focus of discussions with them should be the deity of Jesus Christ.

In Colossians 1:15–19, Paul reveals our Lord's true identity by viewing Him in relation to four things: God, the universe, the unseen world, and the church.

JESUS CHRIST IN RELATION TO GOD

He is the image of the invisible God, the firstborn of all creation. (1:15)

As already noted, the heretics viewed Jesus as one among a series of lesser spirits descending in sequential inferiority from God. Paul refutes that with two powerful descriptions of who Jesus really is. First, Paul describes Him as **the image of the invisible God.** *Eikōn* (**image**) means "image" or "likeness." From it we get our English word *icon,* referring to a statue. It is used in Matthew 22:20 of Caesar's portrait on a coin, and in Revelation 13:14 of the statue of Antichrist.

Although man is also the *eikōn* of God (1 Cor 11:7; cf. Gen 1:26–27), man is not a perfect image of God. Humans are made in God's image in that they have rational personality. Like God, they possess intellect, emotion, and will, by which they are able to think, feel, and choose. We humans are not, however, in God's image morally, because He is holy, and we are sinful. Nor are we created in His image essentially. We do not possess His incommunicable attributes, such as omniscience, omnipotence, immutability, or omnipresence. We are human, not divine.

The Fall marred the original image of God in man. Before the Fall, Adam and Eve were innocent, free of sin, and incapable of dying. They forfeited those qualities when they sinned. When someone puts faith in Christ, however, that person is promised that the image of God will be restored in him or her. "For those whom He foreknew, He also predestined *to become* conformed to the image of His Son" (Rom 8:29; cf. 2 Cor 3:18; Col 3:10). God will make believers sinless like Christ when they enter the final phase of their eternal life.

Unlike man, Jesus Christ is the perfect, absolutely accurate image of God. He did not become the image of God at the incarnation, but has been that from all eternity. Hebrews 1:3 describes Jesus as "the radiance of [God's] glory." Christ reflects God's attributes, as the sun's light reflects the sun. Further, He is said to be "the exact representation of [God's] nature." *Charaktēr* ("exact representation") refers to an engraving tool, or stamp. Jesus is the exact likeness of God. He is in the very form of God (Phil 2:6). That is why He could say, "He who has seen Me has seen the Father" (John 14:9). In Christ, the invisible God became visible, "and we saw His glory, glory as of the only begotten from the Father" (John 1:14).

By using the term *eikōn*, Paul emphasizes that Jesus is both the representation and manifestation of God. He is the full, final, and complete revelation of God. He is God in human flesh. That was His claim (John 8:58; 10:30–33), and the unanimous testimony of Scripture (cf. John 1:1; 20:28; Rom 9:5; Phil 2:6; Col 2:9; Titus 2:13; Heb 1:8; 2 Pet 1:1). To think anything less of Him is blasphemy and gives evidence of a mind blinded by Satan (2 Cor 4:4).

Paul further describes Jesus as **the firstborn of all creation.** From the Arians of the early church to the Jehovah's Witnesses of our own day, those who would deny our Lord's deity have sought support from this phrase. They argue that it speaks of Christ as a created being, and hence He could not be the eternal God. Such an interpretation completely misunderstands the sense of *prōtotokos* (**firstborn**) and ignores the context.

Although *prōtotokos* can mean firstborn chronologically (Luke 2:7), it refers primarily to position, or rank. In both Greek and Jewish culture, the firstborn was the son who had the right of inheritance. He was not necessarily the first one born. Although Esau was born first chronologically, it was Jacob who was the "firstborn" and received the inheritance. Jesus is the One with the right to the inheritance of all creation (cf. Heb 1:2; Rev 5:1–7, 13).

Israel was called God's firstborn in Exodus 4:22 and Jeremiah 31:9. Though not the first people born, they held first place in God's sight among all the nations. In Psalm 89:27, God says of the Messiah, "I also shall make him *My* firstborn," then defines what He means—"the highest of the kings of the earth." In Revelation 1:5, Jesus is called "the firstborn of the dead," even though He was not the first person to be resurrected chronologically. Of all ever raised, He is the preeminent One. Romans 8:29 refers to Him as the firstborn in relation to the church. In all the above cases, firstborn clearly means highest in rank, not first created.

There are many other reasons for rejecting the idea that the use of **firstborn** makes Jesus a created being. Such an interpretation cannot be harmonized with the description of Jesus as *monogenēs* ("only begotten," or "unique") in John 1:18. We might well ask with the early church father Theodoret how, if

Christ was only-begotten, could He be first-begotten? And how, if He were first-begotten, could He be only-begotten? How could He be the first of many in His class, and at the same time the only member of His class? Yet such confusion is inevitable if we assign the meaning "first created" to "firstborn." Further, when the *prōtotokos* is one of the class referred to, the class is plural (cf. Col 1:18; Rom 8:29). Yet, creation is singular. Finally, if Paul meant to convey that Christ was the first created being, why did he not use the Greek word *prōtoktistos,* which means "first created?"

Such an interpretation of *prōtotokos* is also foreign to the context—both the general context of the epistle and the specific context of the passage. If Paul were here teaching that Christ is a created being, he would be agreeing with the central point of the Colossian errorists. They taught that Christ was a created being, the most prominent of the emanations from God. That would run counter to his purpose in writing Colossians, which was to refute the false teachers at Colossae.

Interpreting *prōtotokos* to mean that Christ is a created being is also out of harmony with the immediate context. Paul has just finished describing Christ as the perfect and complete image of God. In the next verse, he refers to Christ as the creator of everything that exists. How then could Christ Himself be a created being? Further, verse 17 states, "He is before all things." Christ existed before anything else was created (cf. Mic 5:2). And only God existed before the creation.

Far from being one of a series of emanations descending from God, Jesus is the perfect image of God. He is the preeminent inheritor over all creation (the genitive *ktiseōs* is better translated "over" than "of"). He both existed before the creation and is exalted in rank above it. Those truths define who Jesus is in relation to God. They also devastate the false teachers' position. But Paul is not finished—his next point undermines another false teaching of the Colossian errorists.

JESUS CHRIST IN RELATION TO THE UNIVERSE

For by Him all things were created, *both* in the heavens and on earth, visible and invisible, whether thrones or dominions or rulers or authorities—all things have been created through Him and for Him. He is before all things, and in Him all things hold together. (1:16–17)

Paul gives three reasons for Jesus' primacy over creation. First, He is the Creator. The false teachers at Colossae viewed Jesus as the first and most important of the emanations from God, but they were convinced it had to be a lesser being much further down the chain who eventually created the material universe. But Paul rejects that blasphemy, insisting that **by Him all things were created.** That truth is affirmed by the apostle John (John 1:3) and the writer of Hebrews (Heb 1:2). Because the Colossian errorists viewed matter as evil, they argued that neither the good God nor a good emanation could have created it. But Paul maintains that Jesus made all things, both in the heavens and on earth, visible and invisible. He refutes the false philosophic dualism of the Colossian heresy. Jesus is God, and He created the material universe.

By studying the creation, one can gain a glimpse of the power, knowledge, and wisdom of the Creator. The sheer size of the universe is staggering. The sun, for example, has a diameter of 864,000 miles (one hundred times that of earth's) and could hold 1.3 million planets the size of earth inside it. The star Betelgeuse, however, has a diameter of 100 million miles, which is larger than the earth's orbit around the sun. It takes sunlight, traveling at 186,000 miles per second, about 8.5 minutes to reach earth. Yet that same light would take more than four years to reach the nearest star, Alpha Centauri, some 24 trillion miles from earth. The galaxy to which our sun belongs, the Milky Way, contains hundreds of billions of stars. And astronomers estimate there are millions, or even billions of galaxies. What they can see leads them to estimate the number of stars in the universe at 10^{25}. That is roughly the number of all the grains of sand on all the world's beaches.

The universe also bears witness to the tremendous wisdom and knowledge of its Creator. Scientists now speak of the Anthropic Principle, "which states that the universe appears to be carefully designed for the well-being of mankind" (Donald B. DeYoung, "Design in Nature: The Anthropic Principle," *Impact,* no. 149 [November 1985]: ii). A change in the rate of Earth's rotation around the sun or on its axis would be catastrophic. The Earth would become either too hot or too cold to support life. If the moon were much nearer to the Earth, huge tides would inundate the continents. A change in the composition of the gases that make up our atmosphere would also be fatal to life. A slight change in the mass of the proton would result in the dissolution of hydrogen atoms. That would result in the destruction of the universe, because hydrogen is its dominant element.

The creation gives mute testimony to the intelligence of its Creator. Max Planck, winner of the Nobel Prize and one of the founders of modern physics, wrote, "According to everything taught by the exact sciences about the immense realm of nature, a certain order prevails—one independent of the human mind ... this order can be formulated in terms of purposeful activity. There is evidence of an intelligent order of the universe to which both man and nature are subservient" (cited in DeYoung, "Design in Nature," iii). It is no wonder that the psalmist wrote, "The heavens are telling of the glory of God; and their expanse is declaring the work of His hands. Day to day pours forth speech, and night to night reveals knowledge. There is no speech, nor are there words; their voice is not heard. Their line has gone out through all the earth, and their utterances to the end of the world" (Ps 19:1–4).

The testimony of nature to its Creator is so clear that it is only through willful unbelief that men can reject it. Paul writes in Romans 1:20, "Since the creation of the world His invisible attributes, His eternal power and divine nature, have been clearly seen, being understood through what has been made, so that they are without excuse." Like those who deny Christ's deity, those who reject Him as Creator give evidence of a mind darkened by sin and blinded by Satan.

Jesus also has primacy over the creation because He is before all things. When the universe began, He already existed (John 1:1–2; 1 John 1:1). He told the Jews in John 8:58, "Before Abraham was born, I am" (not "I was"). He is saying that He is Yahweh, the eternally existing God. The prophet Micah said of Him, "His goings forth are from long ago, from the days of eternity" (Mic 5:2). Revelation 22:13 describes Him as "the Alpha and the Omega, the first and the last, the beginning and the end." As was previously mentioned, anyone existing before time began at the creation is eternal. And only God is eternal.

A third reason for Jesus' primacy over creation is that **in Him all things hold together.** Not only did Jesus create the universe, He also sustains it. He maintains the delicate balance necessary to life's existence. He quite literally holds all things together. He is the power behind every consistency in the universe. He is gravity and centrifugal and centripetal force. He is the One who keeps all the entities in space in their motion. He is the energy of the universe. In his book *The Atom Speaks*, D. Lee Chesnut describes the puzzle of why the nucleus of the atom holds together:

> Consider the dilemma of the nuclear physicist when he finally looks in utter amazement at the pattern he had now drawn of the oxygen nucleus.... For here are eight positively charged protons closely associated together within the confines of this tiny nucleus. With them are eight neutrons—a total of sixteen particles—eight positively charged, eight with no charge.
>
> Earlier physicists had discovered that like charges of electricity and like magnetic poles repel each other, and unlike charges or magnetic poles attract each other. And the entire history of electrical phenomena and electrical equipment had been built up on these principles known as Coulomb's law of electrostatic force and the law of magnetism. What was wrong? What holds the nucleus together? Why doesn't it fly

> apart? And therefore, why do not all atoms fly apart? ([San Diego: Creation-Science Research Center, 1973], 31–33)

Chesnut goes on to describe the experiments performed in the 1920s and 1930s that proved Coulomb's law applied to atomic nuclei. Powerful "atom smashers" were used to fire protons into the nuclei of atoms. Those experiments also gave scientists an understanding of the incredibly powerful force that held protons together within the nucleus. Scientists have dubbed that force the "strong nuclear force," but have no explanation for why it exists. The physicist George Gamow, one of the founders of the Big Bang theory of the origin of the universe, wrote,

> The fact that we live in a world in which practically every object is a potential nuclear explosive, without being blown to bits, is due to the extreme difficulties that attend the starting of a nuclear reaction. (cited in Chesnut, *The Atom Speaks*, 38)

Karl K. Darrow, a physicist at the Bell (AT&T) Laboratories, agrees:

> You grasp what this implies. It implies that all the massive nuclei have no right to be alive at all. Indeed, they should never have been created, and, if created, they should have blown up instantly. Yet here they all are.... Some inflexible inhibition is holding them relentlessly together. The nature

> of the inhibition is also a secret ... one thus far reserved by Nature for herself. (cited in Chesnut, *The Atom Speaks*, 38)

One day in the future God will dissolve the strong nuclear force. Peter describes that day as the one when "the heavens will pass away with a roar and the elements will be destroyed with intense heat, and the earth and its works will be burned up" (2 Pet 3:10). With the strong nuclear force no longer operative, Coulomb's law will take effect, and the nuclei of atoms will fly apart. The universe will literally explode. Until that time, we can be thankful that Christ "upholds all things by the word of His power" (Heb 1:3). Jesus Christ must be God. He made the universe, existed outside and before it, and preserves it.

JESUS CHRIST IN RELATION TO THE UNSEEN WORLD

... whether thrones or dominions or rulers or authorities ... (1:16*b*)

Thrones, dominions, rulers, and **authorities** refer to the various ranks of angels. Far from being an angel, as the Colossian errorists taught, Christ created the angels. The writer of Hebrews also makes a clear distinction between Christ and the angels: "Of the angels *He says,* 'WHO MAKES HIS ANGELS WINDS, AND

HIS MINISTERS A FLAME OF FIRE.' But of the Son *He says*, 'YOUR THRONE, O GOD, IS FOREVER AND EVER, AND THE RIGHTEOUS SCEPTER IS THE SCEPTER OF HIS KINGDOM'" (Heb 1:7–8). Jesus has been exalted "far above all rule and authority and power and dominion, and every name that is named, not only in this age but also in the one to come" (Eph 1:21). As a result, "At the name of Jesus EVERY KNEE WILL BOW, of those who are in heaven and on earth and under the earth" (Phil 2:10). With that truth the apostle Peter agrees: "[Christ] is at the right hand of God, having gone into heaven, after angels and authorities and powers had been subjected to Him" (1 Pet 3:22).

Scripture is clear that Jesus is not an angel, but the Creator of the angels. He is above the angels, who in fact worship Him and are under His authority. Jesus' relation to the unseen world, like His relation to the visible universe, proves He is God.

JESUS CHRIST IN RELATION TO THE CHURCH

He is also head of the body, the church; and He is the beginning, the firstborn from the dead, so that He Himself will come to have first place in everything. (1:18)

Paul presents four great truths in this verse about Christ's relation to the church.

CHRIST IS THE HEAD OF THE CHURCH

There are many metaphors used in Scripture to describe the church. It is called a family, a kingdom, a vineyard, a flock, a building, and a bride. But the most profound metaphor, one having no Old Testament equivalent, is that of a Body. The church is a Body, and Christ is the head of the Body. This concept is not used in the sense of the head of a company, but rather looks at the church as a living organism, inseparably tied together by the living Christ. He controls every part of it and gives it life and direction. His life lived out through all the members provides the unity of the Body (cf. 1 Cor 12:12–20). He energizes and coordinates the diversity within the Body, a diversity of spiritual gifts and ministries (1 Cor 12:4–13). He also directs the Body's mutuality, as the individual members serve and support each other (1 Cor 12:15–27).

Christ is not an angel who serves the church (cf. Heb 1:14). He is the head of His church.

CHRIST IS THE SOURCE OF THE CHURCH

Archē (**beginning**) is used here in the twofold sense of source and primacy. The church has its origins in Jesus. God "chose us in Him before the foundation of the world" (Eph 1:4). It is He who gives life to His church. His sacrificial death and resurrection on our behalf provided our new life. As head of the Body, Jesus holds the chief position, or highest rank in the church. As the beginning, He is its originator.

CHRIST IS THE FIRSTBORN FROM THE DEAD

Firstborn again translates *prōtotokos*. Of all those who have been raised from the dead, or ever will be, Christ is the highest in rank.

CHRIST IS THE PREEMINENT ONE

As a result of His death and resurrection, Jesus has come to have first place in everything. Paul summarizes for emphasis in verse 18. He wants to drive home the point as forcefully as he can that Jesus is not merely another emanation from God. Because

> He humbled Himself by becoming obedient to the point of death, even death on a cross ... God highly exalted Him, and bestowed on Him the name which is above

> every name, so that at the name of Jesus EVERY KNEE WILL BOW, of those who are in heaven and on earth and under the earth, and that every tongue will confess that Jesus Christ is Lord, to the glory of God the Father. (Phil 2:8–11)

Jesus reigns supreme over the visible world, the unseen world, and the church. Paul sums up his argument in verse 19: **For it was the *Father's* good pleasure for all the fullness to dwell in Him.** *Plērōma* (**fullness**) was a term used by the later Gnostics to refer to the divine powers and attributes, which they believed were divided among the various emanations. That is likely the sense in which the Colossian errorists used the term. Paul counters that false teaching by stating that all the fullness of deity is not spread out in small doses to a group of spirits, but fully dwells in Christ alone (cf. 2:9). The commentator J. B. Lightfoot wrote about Paul's use of *plērōma*,

> On the one hand, in relation to Deity, He is the visible image of the invisible God. He is not only the chief manifestation of the Divine nature: He exhausts the Godhead manifested. In Him resides the totality of the Divine powers and attributes. For this totality Gnostic teachers had a technical term, the *pleroma* or *plenitude*.... In contrast to their doctrine, [Paul] asserts and repeats the assertion, that the pleroma abides absolutely and wholly in Christ as the Word of God. The entire light is concentrated in Him. (*St. Paul's*

Epistles to the Colossians and to Philemon [1879; reprint, Grand Rapids: Zondervan, 1959], 102)

Paul tells the Colossians they do not need angels to help them get saved. Rather in Christ, and Him alone, they are complete (2:10). Christians share in His fullness: "For of His fullness we have all received, and grace upon grace" (John 1:16). All the fullness of Christ becomes available to believers.

What should the response be to the glorious truths about Christ in this passage? The Puritan John Owen astutely wrote,

> The revelation made of Christ in the blessed gospel is far more excellent, more glorious, more filled with rays of divine wisdom and goodness than the whole creation, and the just comprehension of it, if attainable, can contain or afford. Without this knowledge, the mind of man, however priding itself in other inventions and discoveries, is wrapped up in darkness and confusion.
>
> This therefore deserves the severest of our thoughts, the best of our meditations, and our utmost diligence in them. For if our future blessedness shall consist in living where He is, and beholding of His glory, what better preparation can there be for it than a constant previous contemplation of that glory as revealed in the gospel, that by a view of it we may be gradually transformed into the same glory? (John Owen, *The Glory of Christ* [reprint, Chicago: Moody, 1949], 25–26)

05

RECONCILED TO GOD

COLOSSIANS 1:20–23

And through Him to reconcile all things to Himself, having made peace through the blood of His cross; through Him, *I say,* whether things on earth or things in heaven.

And although you were formerly alienated and hostile in mind, *engaged* in evil deeds, yet He has now reconciled you in His fleshly body through death, in order to present you before Him holy and blameless and beyond reproach—if indeed you continue in the faith firmly established and steadfast, and not moved away from the hope of the gospel that you have heard, which was proclaimed in all creation under heaven, and of which I, Paul, was made a minister. (1:20–23)

The word *reconcile* is one of the most significant and descriptive terms in all of Scripture. It is one of five key words used in the New Testament to describe the richness of salvation in Christ, along with *justification, redemption, forgiveness,* and *adoption.*

In justification, the sinner stands before God guilty and condemned, but is declared righteous (Rom 8:33). In redemption, the sinner stands before God as a slave, but is granted his freedom (Rom 6:18–22). In forgiveness, the sinner stands before God as a debtor, but the debt is paid and forgotten (Eph 1:7). In reconciliation, the sinner stands before God as an enemy, but becomes His friend (2 Cor 5:18–20). In adoption, the sinner stands before God as a stranger, but is made a son (Eph 1:5). A complete understanding of the doctrine of salvation would involve a detailed study of each of those terms. In Colossians 1:20–23, Paul gives a concise look at reconciliation.

The verb *katallassō* (**to reconcile**) means "to change" or "exchange." Its New Testament usage speaks of a change in a relationship. In 1 Corinthians 7:11 it refers to a woman being reconciled to her husband. In its other two New Testament usages, Romans 5:10, and 2 Corinthians 5:18–20, it speaks of God and man being reconciled. When people change from being at enmity with each other to being at peace, they are said to be reconciled. When the Bible speaks of reconciliation, then, it refers to the restoration of a right relationship between God and man.

There is another term for reconcile that is used in Colossians 1:20, 22—*apokatallassō*. It is a compound word, made up of the basic word for reconcile, *katallassō,* with a preposition added to intensify the meaning. It means thoroughly, completely, or totally reconciled. Paul no doubt used this stronger term in Colossians as a counterattack against the false teachers. Because they held that Christ was merely another spirit being emanating from God, they also denied the possibility of man's being reconciled to God by Christ alone. In refuting that denial, Paul emphasizes that there is total, complete, and full reconciliation through the Lord Jesus. Inasmuch as He possesses all the fullness of deity (1:19; 2:9), Jesus is able to fully reconcile sinful men and women to God (1:20).

Paul defends Christ's sufficiency to reconcile men to God by discussing four aspects of reconciliation: the plan of reconciliation, the means of reconciliation, the aim of reconciliation, and the evidence of reconciliation.

THE PLAN OF RECONCILIATION

… and through Him to reconcile all things to Himself, having made peace through the blood of His cross; through Him, *I say,* whether things on earth or things in heaven.

And although you were formerly alienated and hostile in mind, *engaged* in evil deeds … (1:20–21)

God's ultimate plan for the universe is **to reconcile all things to Himself** through Jesus Christ. When His work of creation was finished, "God saw all that He had made, and behold, it was very good" (Gen 1:31). God's good creation, however, was soon marred by man's sin. The Fall resulted not only in fatal and damning tragedy for the human race, but also affected the entire creation. Sin destroyed the perfect harmony between creatures, and between all creation and the Creator. The creation was "subjected to futility" (Rom 8:20) and "groans and suffers the pains of childbirth together until now" (Rom 8:22). One evidence of that is the Second Law of Thermodynamics, which indicates that the universe is losing its usable energy. If God did not intervene, the universe would eventually suffer a heat death—all available energy would be used up, and the universe would become uniformly cold and dark.

We live on a cursed earth in a cursed universe. Both are under the baleful influence of Satan, who is both "the god of this world" (2 Cor 4:4), and "the prince of the power of the air" (Eph 2:2). The devastating effects of the curse and satanic influence will reach a terrifying climax in the events of the Tribulation. Some of the various bowl, trumpet, and seal judgments are demonic, others represent natural phenomena gone wild as God lets loose His wrath. At the culmination of that time of destruction and chaos, Christ returns and sets up His kingdom. During His millennial reign, the effects of the curse will begin to be reversed. The Bible gives us a glimpse of what the restored creation will be like.

There will be dramatic changes in the animal world. In Isaiah we learn that

> the wolf will dwell with the lamb, and the leopard will lie down with the young goat, and the calf and the young lion and the fatling together; and a little boy will lead them. Also the cow and the bear will graze, their young will lie down together,

> and the lion will eat straw like the ox. The nursing child will play by the hole of the cobra, and the weaned child will put his hand on the viper's den. They will not hurt or destroy in all My holy mountain. (Isa 11:6–9)

> "The wolf and the lamb will graze together, and the lion will eat straw like the ox; and dust will be the serpent's food. They will do no evil or harm in all My holy mountain," says the LORD. (Isa 65:25)

The changes in the animal world will be paralleled by changes in the earth and the solar system:

> Then the moon will be abashed and the sun ashamed, for the LORD of hosts will reign on Mount Zion and in Jerusalem, and *His* glory will be before His elders. (Isa 24:23)

> The light of the moon will be as the light of the sun, and the light of the sun will be seven times *brighter*, like the light of seven days, on the day the LORD binds up the fracture of His people and heals the bruise He has inflicted. (Isa 30:26)

> No longer will you have the sun for light by day, nor for brightness will the moon give you light; but you will have the LORD for an everlasting light, and your God for your glory. Your sun will no longer set, nor will your moon wane; for you will have the LORD for an everlasting light. (Isa 60:19–20)

Tremendous, dramatic changes will mark the reconciliation of the world to God. Paul writes, "The creation itself also will be set free from its slavery to corruption" (Rom 8:21). God and the creation will be reconciled; the curse of Genesis 3 will be removed. We might say that God will make friends with the universe again. The universe will be restored to a proper relationship with its Creator. Finally, after the millennial kingdom, there will indeed be a new heaven and a new earth, as both Peter and John indicate:

> According to His promise we are looking for new heavens and a new earth, in which righteousness dwells. (2 Pet 3:13)

> I saw a new heaven and a new earth; for the first heaven and the first earth passed away. (Rev 21:1)

The Lord will make everything new.

Paul again takes direct aim at the false philosophical dualism of the Colossian heretics. They taught that all matter was evil and spirit was good. In their scheme, God did not create the physical universe, and He certainly would not wish to be reconciled to it. Paul declares that God will indeed reconcile the material world to Himself, and further, that He will do it through His Son, Jesus Christ. Far from being a spirit emanation unconcerned with evil matter, Jesus is the agent through which God will accomplish the reconciliation of the universe. The German theologian Erich Sauer comments,

> The offering on Golgotha extends its influence into universal history. The salvation of mankind is only *one part* of the world-embracing counsels of God.... The "heavenly things" also will be cleansed through Christ's sacrifice of Himself (Heb 9:23). A "cleansing" of the heavenly places is required if on no other ground than that they have been the dwelling of fallen spirits (Eph 6:12; 2:2), and because Satan, their chief, has for ages had access to the highest regions of the heavenly world ... the other side becomes this side; eternity transfigures time and this earth, the chief scene of the redemption, becomes the Residence of the universal kingdom of God. (*The Triumph of the Crucified* [Grand Rapids: Eerdmans, 1960], 179, 180 [italics in original])

Some have imagined **all things** to include fallen men and fallen angels, and on that basis have argued for universalism, the ultimate salvation of everyone. By so doing they overlook a fundamental rule of interpretation, the *analogia Scriptura*. That principle teaches that no passage of Scripture, properly interpreted, will contradict any other passage. When we let Scripture interpret Scripture, it is clear that by all things Paul means all things for whom reconciliation is possible. That fallen angels and unregenerate men will spend eternity in hell is the emphatic teaching of Scripture. Our Lord will one day say to unbelievers, "Depart from Me, accursed ones, into the eternal fire which has been prepared for the devil and his angels," and they "will go away into eternal punishment" (Matt 25:41, 46). In Revelation 20:10–15, the apostle John writes,

> The devil who deceived them was thrown into the lake of fire and brimstone, where the beast and the false prophet are also; and they will be tormented day and night forever and ever.
>
> Then I saw a great white throne and Him who sat upon it, from whose presence earth and heaven fled away, and no place was found for them. And I saw the dead, the great and the small, standing before the throne, and books were opened; and another book was opened, which is *the book* of life; and the dead were judged from the things which were written in the books, according to their deeds. And the sea gave up the dead which were in it, and death and Hades gave up the dead which were in them; and they were judged, every one *of them* according to their deeds. Then death and Hades were thrown into the lake of fire. This is the second death, the lake of fire. And if anyone's name was not found written in the book of life, he was thrown into the lake of fire.

On the other hand, there is a sense in which even fallen angels and unredeemed men will be reconciled to God for judgment—but only in the sense of submitting to Him for final sentencing. Their relationship to Him will change from that of enemies to that of the judged. They will be sentenced to hell, unable any longer to pollute God's creation. They will be stripped of their power and forced to bow in submission to God. Paul writes in Colossians 2:15 that after Christ "disarmed the rulers and authorities [fallen angels], He made a public display of them, having triumphed over them." Because of Christ's victory, "the God of peace will soon crush Satan under your feet" (Rom 16:20). And "at the name of Jesus EVERY KNEE WILL BOW, of those who are in heaven and on earth and under the earth" (Phil 2:10). God has elevated Christ to a position above all things, whether things on earth or things in heaven. Paul wrote to the Ephesians that God "raised Him from the dead and seated Him at His right hand in the heavenly *places*, far above all rule and authority and power and dominion, and every name that is named, not only in this age but also in the one to come. And He put all things in subjection under His feet" (Eph 1:20–22).

Though in the sacrifice of Christ, God made provision for the world (cf. John 3:16; 1 John 2:2), all persons will not be reconciled to God in the saving sense of being redeemed. The benefits of Christ's atonement are applied only to the elect, who alone come to saving faith in Him.

From God's general plan to reconcile all things to Himself, Paul turns to the specific reconciliation of believers like the Colossians. That they had been reconciled was evidence enough that Christ was sufficient to reconcile men and women to God. Their reconciliation foreshadowed the ultimate reconciliation of the universe.

To impress on them Christ's power to reconcile men to God, Paul reminds the Colossians of what they were like before their reconciliation. They **were formerly alienated and hostile in mind, *engaged* in evil deeds.** *Apallotrioō* (**alienated**) means "estranged," "cut off," or "separated." Before their reconciliation, the Colossians were completely estranged from God. In a similar passage, Paul writes, "You were at that time separate from Christ, excluded from the commonwealth of Israel, and strangers to the covenants of promise, having no hope and without God in the world. But now in Christ Jesus you who formerly were far off have been brought near by the blood of Christ" (Eph 2:12–13). Non-Christians are detached from God because of sin; there is no such thing as an "innocent heathen." All unbelievers suffer separation from God unless they receive the reconciliation provided in Jesus Christ.

The Colossians had also been **hostile in mind.** *Echthros* (**hostile**) could also be translated "hateful." Unbelievers are not only alienated from God by condition, but also hateful of God by attitude. They hate Him and resent His holy standards and commands because they are ***engaged* in evil deeds.** Scripture teaches that unbelievers "loved the darkness rather than the Light, for their deeds were evil. For everyone who does evil hates the Light, and does not come to the Light for fear that his deeds will be exposed" (John

3:19–20). Their problem is not ignorance, but willful love of sin.

> Even though they knew God, they did not honor Him as God or give thanks, but they became futile in their speculations, and their foolish heart was darkened. Professing to be wise, they became fools, and exchanged the glory of the incorruptible God for an image in the form of corruptible man and of birds and four-footed animals and crawling creatures.
>
> Therefore God gave them over in the lusts of their hearts to impurity, so that their bodies would be dishonored among them. (Rom 1:21–24)

Although "that which is known about God is evident within them; for God made it evident to them" (Rom 1:19), they "suppress the truth in unrighteousness" (Rom 1:18). As Isaiah wrote to wayward Israel, "Your iniquities have made a separation between you and your God, and your sins have hidden *His* face from you, so that He does not hear" (Isa 59:2). Sin is the root cause of man's alienation from God. Because God cannot fellowship with sin (cf. Hab 1:13; 1 John 1:6), it is sin that needs to be dealt with before God and man can be reconciled.

The question arises as to whether man is reconciled to God, or God to man. There is a sense in which both occur. Since "the mind set on the flesh is hostile toward God" (Rom 8:7), and "those who are in the flesh cannot please God" (Rom 8:8), reconciliation cannot take place until man is transformed. "Therefore if anyone is in Christ, *he is* a new creature; the old things passed away; behold, new things have come. Now all *these* things are from God, who reconciled us to Himself through Christ" (2 Cor 5:17–18).

There is also God's side to reconciliation. From His holy perspective, His just wrath against sin must be appeased. Far from being the harmless, tolerant grandfather that many today imagine Him to be, God "takes vengeance on His adversaries, and He reserves wrath for His enemies" (Nah 1:2). "At His wrath the earth quakes, and the nations cannot endure His indignation" (Jer 10:10). The one who refuses to obey the Son will find that "the wrath of God abides on him" (John 3:36). Because of their sin, "the wrath of God comes upon the sons of disobedience" (Eph 5:6). Man and God could never be reconciled unless God's wrath was appeased. The provision for that took place through Christ's sacrifice. "Much more then, having now been justified by His blood, we shall be saved from the wrath *of God* through Him" (Rom 5:9). It is "Jesus, who rescues us from the wrath to come" (1 Thess 1:10). He bore the full fury of God's wrath against our sins (cf. 2 Cor 5:21; 1 Pet 2:24). After all, "God has not destined us for wrath, but for obtaining salvation through our Lord Jesus Christ" (1 Thess 5:9).

Christ's death on the cross reconciled us to God (Eph 2:16), something we could never have done on our own. In Romans 5:6–10, Paul gives four reasons for that. First, lack of strength: "we were still helpless" (v. 6). Second, lack of merit: we were "the ungodly" (v. 6). Third, lack of righteousness: "we were yet sinners" (v. 8). Finally, lack of peace with God: "we were enemies" (v. 10). It is only through the atoning work of the Lord Jesus Christ that anyone can receive reconciliation (v. 11).

THE MEANS OF RECONCILIATION

... having made peace through the blood of His cross ... He has now reconciled you in His fleshly body through death ... (1:20*b*, 1:22*a*)

Those two phrases sum up the specific means whereby Christ effected our reconciliation with God. Paul says first that Christ made peace between God and man through the blood of His cross. Blood speaks metaphorically of His atonement. It connects Christ's death with the Old Testament sacrificial system (cf. 1 Pet 1:18–19). It is also a term that graphically notes violent death, such as that suffered by the sacrificial animals. The countless thousands of animals sacrificed under the Old Covenant pointed ahead to the violent, blood-shedding death the final sacrificial Lamb would suffer. The writer of Hebrews informs us that "bodies of those animals whose blood is brought into the holy place by the high priest *as an offering* for sin, are burned outside the camp. Therefore Jesus also, that He might sanctify the people through His own blood, suffered outside the gate" (Heb 13:11–12).

The reference to Christ's blood again stresses the link between His violent death and the violent deaths of the animals sacrificed under the Old Covenant. Unlike many of them, however, Jesus did not bleed to death (cf. John 19:34). No man took His life. He was not a helpless victim, but willingly offered up His life to God.

> For this reason the Father loves Me, because I lay down My life so that I may take it again. No one has taken it away from Me, but I lay it down on My own initiative. I have authority to lay it down, and I have authority to take it up again. This commandment I received from My Father. (John 10:17–18)

Jesus chose the moment of His death: "Therefore when Jesus had received the sour wine, He said, "It is finished!" And He bowed His head and gave up His spirit" (John 19:30).

There is nothing mystical, however, about the blood of Christ. It saves us only in the sense that His death was the sacrificial death of the final Lamb. It was that death that reconciled us to God (Rom 5:10).

Proper biblical teaching on the blood of Christ simply is that His physical blood has no magical or mystical saving power. It is not some supernaturally preserved form of the actual blood of Christ that literally washes believers of their sin. The blood of Christ is applied to the believer in a symbolic sense, by faith, in the same way that we "see" Christ by faith, and we are seated with Him in the heavenlies—not in a physical sense.

How could the red and white corpuscles be literally applied to believers in salvation? To our physical bodies? Could it be otherwise with literal blood? Where is that literal, tangible blood kept? How much of it is applied, and why is it not used up? To one degree or another, we must acknowledge that there is symbolism in what Scripture says about the blood. Otherwise we will wind up with an obviously unbiblical doctrine like transubstantiation to explain how literal blood can be applied to all believers for salvation. (I have recently heard that some believe the blood of Jesus is kept in a bottle in heaven to be literally used in some way to apply to the soul!)

A strictly physical interpretation of what Scripture says about the blood of Christ cannot adequately deal with such passages as John 6:53–54: "Truly, truly, I say to you, unless you eat the flesh of the Son of Man and drink His blood, you have no life in yourselves.

He who eats My flesh and drinks My blood has eternal life, and I will raise him up on the last day."

It would be equally hard to explain how physical blood is meant in Matthew 23:30–35 ("We would not have been partakers with them in *shedding* the blood of the prophets"); 27:24–25 ("His blood shall be on us and on our children"); Acts 5:28 ("[you] intend to bring this man's blood upon us"); 18:6 ("Your blood *be* on your own heads"); 20:26, 28 ("I am innocent of the blood of all men"); and 1 Corinthians 10:16 ("Is not the cup of blessing which we bless a sharing in the blood of Christ?").

The literal blood of Christ ran into the dirt and dust, and nothing in Scripture hints that it now exists in any tangible or visible form. Communion wine does not change into blood. There is no way the actual blood of Christ could be applied to all of us. We must acknowledge at some point that the sprinkling with blood under the New Covenant is symbolic.

"Without shedding of blood there is no forgiveness" (Heb 9:22). I affirm that truth and have never denied it. But the "shedding of blood" in Scripture is an expression that means much more than just bleeding. It refers to violent sacrificial death. If just bleeding could buy salvation, why did not Jesus simply bleed without dying? Of course, He had to die to be the perfect sacrifice, and without His death our redemption could not have been purchased by His blood.

The meaning of Scripture in this matter is not all that difficult to understand. Romans 5:9–10 clarifies the point; those two verses side by side show that to be "justified by His blood" (v. 9) is the same as being "reconciled to God through the death of His Son" (v. 10). The critical element in salvation is the sacrificial death of Christ on our behalf. The shedding of His blood was the visible manifestation of His life being poured out in sacrifice, and Scripture consistently uses the term "shedding of blood" as a metonym for atoning death. (A metonym is a figure of speech in which the part is used to represent or designate the whole.)

Bloodshed was God's design for all Old Testament sacrifices. They were bled to death rather than clubbed or burnt. God designed that sacrificial death was to occur with blood loss as a vivid manifestation of life being poured out ("the life of the flesh is in the blood"). Nevertheless, those who were too poor to bring animals for sacrifices were allowed to bring one-tenth of an ephah (about two quarts) of fine flour instead (Lev 5:11). Their sins were covered just as surely as the sins of those who could afford to offer a lamb, goat, turtledoves, or pigeons (Lev 5:6–7). Christ's blood was precious—but as precious as it was, only when it was poured out in death could the penalty of sin be paid.

Thus, if Christ had bled without dying, salvation would not have been purchased. In that sense, it is not His blood but His death that saves us. And when

Scripture talks about the shedding of blood, the point is not mere bleeding, but dying by violence as a sacrifice. That is not heresy, and nothing in Protestant church history would support the notion that it is. The only major group to insist that the application of the blood is literal is the Roman Catholic Church.

Christ died not only as a sacrifice, but also as our substitute. He has now reconciled you in His fleshly body through death. In Romans 8:3, Paul tells us that God sent "His own Son in the likeness of sinful flesh and *as an offering* for sin, He condemned sin in the flesh." He took the place of sinners, dying a substitutionary death that paid the full penalty for the sin of all who believe. This death satisfied God's wrath. Once again Paul hammers away at the false teaching of the Colossian heretics that Christ was a mere spirit being. On the contrary, Paul insists, He died as a man for men. Were that not true, there could be no reconciliation for any person.

THE AIM OF RECONCILIATION

... in order to present you before Him holy and blameless and beyond reproach ... (1:22*b*)

God's ultimate goal in reconciliation is to present His elect holy and pure before Him. Paul expressed a similar desire for the Corinthians: "I am jealous for you with a godly jealousy; for I betrothed you to one husband, so that to Christ I might present you *as* a pure virgin" (2 Cor 11:2). Jude tells us that we will one day "stand in the presence of His glory blameless with great joy" (Jude 24). Such purification is necessary if sinners are to stand in the presence of a holy God.

Holy (*hagios*) means to be separated from sin and set apart to God. It has to do with the believer's relationship with Him. As a result of a faith union with Jesus Christ, God sees Christians as holy as His Son. God "chose us in Him before the foundation of the world, that we would be holy and blameless before Him" (Eph 1:4). "He made Him who knew no sin *to be* sin on our behalf, that we might become the righteousness of God in Him" (2 Cor 5:21).

Blameless (*amōmos*) means without blemish. It was used in the Septuagint to speak of sacrificial animals (Num 6:14). It is used in the New Testament to refer to Christ as the spotless Lamb of God (Heb 9:14; 1 Pet 1:19). In reference to ourselves, reconciliation gives us a blameless character.

Beyond reproach (*anegklētos*) goes beyond blameless. It means not only that we are without blemish, but also that no one can bring a charge against us (cf. Rom 8:33). Satan, the accuser of the brethren (Rev 12:10), cannot make a charge stick against those whom Christ has reconciled.

Christ's reconciliation makes believers holy, blameless, and beyond reproach **before Him.** God sees us now as we will be in heaven when we are glorified. He views us clothed with the very righteousness of Jesus Christ. The process of spiritual growth involves becoming in practice what we are in reality before God. We "have put on the new self" and that new self "is being renewed to a true knowledge according to the image of the One who created him" (Col 3:10). The Christian life involves "beholding as in a mirror the glory of the Lord [which covers us before God, and] being transformed into the same image from glory to glory, just as from the Lord, the Spirit" (2 Cor 3:18).

THE EVIDENCE OF RECONCILIATION

... if indeed you continue in the faith firmly established and steadfast, and not moved away from the hope of the gospel that you have heard, which was proclaimed in all creation under heaven, and of which I, Paul, was made a minister. (1:23)

One of the most sobering truths in the Bible is that not all who profess to be Christians are in fact saved. Our Lord warned, "Many will say to Me on that day, 'Lord, Lord, did we not prophesy in Your name, and in Your name cast out demons, and in Your name perform many miracles?' And then I will declare to them, 'I never knew you; DEPART FROM ME, YOU WHO PRACTICE LAWLESSNESS'" (Matt 7:22–23).

Of all the marks of a genuine Christian presented in Scripture, none is more significant than the one Paul mentions here. People give evidence of being truly reconciled when they **continue in the faith firmly established and steadfast.** The Bible repeatedly testifies that those who are truly reconciled will continue in the faith. In the parable of the soils, Jesus described those represented by the rocky soil as "those who, when they hear, receive the word with joy; and these have no *firm* root; they believe for a while, and in time of temptation fall away" (Luke 8:13). By falling away they gave evidence that they were never truly saved. In John 8:31, "Jesus was saying to those Jews who had believed Him, 'If you continue in My word, *then* you are truly disciples of Mine.'" Speaking of apostates, the apostle John writes in 1 John 2:19, "They went out from us, but they were not *really* of us; for if they had been of us, they would have remained with us; but *they went out,* so that it would be shown that they all are not of us."

After hearing some difficult and challenging teaching from Him, many of Jesus' so-called disciples "withdrew and were not walking with Him anymore" (John 6:66). By so doing, they gave evidence that they had never truly been His disciples. Perseverance is the hallmark of the true saint. (I discuss the issue further in my books *The Gospel According to Jesus* [Grand Rapids: Zondervan, 1988] and *Saved Without a Doubt* [Wheaton, Ill.: Victor, 1992].)

Lest there be any confusion about what they were to continue in, Paul specifies the content of their faith as **the gospel that you have heard, which was proclaimed in all creation under heaven, and of which I, Paul, was made a minister.** The Colossians are to hold fast to the apostolic gospel they had heard; the gospel that had been proclaimed throughout the world; the gospel of which Paul was a minister, commissioned to preach. Those who, like the Colossian errorists, preach any other gospel stand cursed before God (Gal 1:8).

Perhaps no passage stresses the vital importance of reconciliation more than 2 Corinthians 5:17–21:

> If anyone is in Christ, *he is* a new creature; the old things passed away; behold, new things have come. Now all *these* things are from God, who reconciled us to Himself through Christ and gave us the ministry of reconciliation, namely, that God was in Christ reconciling the world to Himself, not counting their trespasses against them, and He has committed to us the word of reconciliation.
>
> Therefore, we are ambassadors for Christ, as though God were making an appeal through us; we beg you on behalf of Christ, be reconciled to God. He made Him who knew no sin *to be* sin on our behalf, so that we might become the righteousness of God in Him.

In that powerful text we can discern five truths about reconciliation. First, reconciliation transforms men: "If anyone is in Christ, *he is* a new creature; the old things passed away; behold, new things have come" (v. 17). Second, it appeases God's wrath: "He made Him who knew no sin *to be* sin on our behalf, so that we might become the righteousness of God in Him" (v. 21). Third, it comes through Christ: "All *these* things are from God, who reconciled us to Himself through Christ" (v. 18). Fourth, it is available to all who believe: "God was in Christ reconciling the world to Himself" (v. 19). Finally, every believer has been given the ministry of proclaiming the message of reconciliation: God "gave us the ministry of reconciliation" (v. 18), and "He has committed to us the word of reconciliation" (v. 19).

God sends His people forth as ambassadors into a fallen, lost world, bearing unbelievably good news. People everywhere are hopelessly lost and doomed, cut off from God by sin. But God has provided the means of reconciliation through the death of His Son. Our mission is to plead with people to receive that reconciliation, before it is too late. Paul's attitude, expressed in verse 20, should mark every Christian: "Therefore, we are ambassadors for Christ, as though God were making an appeal through us; we beg you on behalf of Christ, be reconciled to God."

06

PAUL'S VIEW OF THE MINISTRY

COLOSSIANS 1:24–29

Now I rejoice in my sufferings for your sake, and in my flesh I do my share on behalf of His body, which is the church, in filling up what is lacking in Christ's afflictions. Of *this church* I was made a minister according to the stewardship from God bestowed on me for your benefit, so that I might fully carry out the *preaching of* the word of God, *that is,* the mystery which has been hidden from the *past* ages and generations, but has now been manifested to His saints, to whom God willed to make known what is the riches of the glory of this mystery among the Gentiles, which is Christ in you, the hope of glory. We proclaim Him, admonishing every man and teaching every man with all wisdom, so that we may present every man complete in Christ. For this purpose also I labor, striving according to His power, which mightily works within me. (1:24–29)

The ministry is a topic that was dear to the heart of the apostle Paul, and it is a frequent theme in his letters. He never lost the sense of wonder that God would call him to the ministry, and he never tired of talking about it. Toward the end of his life, he wrote to his protege and fellow minister Timothy, "I thank Christ Jesus our Lord, who has strengthened me, because He considered me faithful, putting me into service, even though I was formerly a blasphemer and a persecutor and a violent aggressor" (1 Tim 1:12–13).

Like Jeremiah, who spoke of the Word of God as a burning fire in his bones (Jer 20:9), Paul felt compelled to carry out his ministry. To the Corinthians he wrote, "For if I preach the gospel, I have nothing to boast of, for I am under compulsion; for woe is me if I do not preach the gospel" (1 Cor 9:16).

Paul often spoke of his ministry when he needed to establish his authority and credibility. That was his aim in this passage. Colossians was written in part as a polemic against false teachers, and it was essential for Paul to defend his authority to speak for God. Otherwise, the false teachers would have dismissed what he wrote as merely his own opinion. Having begun the epistle with a statement of his apostolic authority (1:1), Paul now gives a detailed look at the divine character of his ministry. He recites eight aspects of that ministry: the source of the ministry, the spirit of the ministry, the suffering of the ministry, the scope of the ministry, the subject of the ministry, the style of the ministry, the sum of the ministry, and the strength of the ministry.

THE SOURCE OF THE MINISTRY

... the gospel ... of which I, Paul, was made a minister.... Of *this church* I was made a minister according to the stewardship from God bestowed on me for your benefit ... (1:23*c*, 25*a*)

Paul closed out the last section by describing the content of the Colossians' faith, namely the gospel, the saving truth of which he **was made a minister** (1:23). In 1:25 he repeats the thought, saying again that he **was made a minister** of Christ's church. The source of his ministry was God.

Becoming a minister of Jesus Christ was not what Saul of Tarsus planned to do with his life. On the contrary, he appeared headed for the upper echelons of Judaism. His credentials were impressive. He was "circumcised the eighth day, of the nation of Israel, of the tribe of Benjamin, a Hebrew of Hebrews; as to the Law, a Pharisee; as to zeal, a persecutor of the church; as to the righteousness which is in the Law, found blameless" (Phil 3:5–6). Although born in Tarsus, he was brought up in Jerusalem, "educated under Gamaliel, strictly according to the law of our fathers, being zealous for God" (Acts 22:3). He said, "[I was] advancing in Judaism beyond many of my contemporaries among my countrymen, being more extremely zealous for my ancestral traditions"

(Gal 1:14). It was that zeal that led him to become a persecutor of Christians.

New Testament readers first meet Paul under his Jewish name, Saul, at Stephen's martyrdom. "When they had driven him out of the city, they *began* stoning *him*; and the witnesses laid aside their robes at the feet of a young man named Saul" (Acts 7:58). Not content with a supporting role, he quickly became the leading persecutor of the church: "Now Saul, still breathing threats and murder against the disciples of the Lord, went to the high priest, and asked for letters from him to the synagogues at Damascus, so that if he found any belonging to the Way, both men and women, he might bring them bound to Jerusalem" (Acts 9:1–2). He "persecuted this Way to the death, binding and putting both men and women into prisons" (Acts 22:4). As he described it in his testimony before King Agrippa,

> So then, I thought to myself that I had to do many things hostile to the name of Jesus of Nazareth. And this is just what I did in Jerusalem; not only did I lock up many of the saints in prisons, having received authority from the chief priests, but also when they were being put to death I cast my vote against them. And as I punished them often in all the synagogues, I tried to force them to blaspheme; and being furiously enraged at them, I kept pursuing them even to foreign cities. (Acts 26:9–11)

It was while engaged in his one-man crusade to wipe out the church that he had the experience which turned his world upside down:

> As I was journeying to Damascus with the authority and commission of the chief priests, at midday, O King, I saw on the way a light from heaven, brighter than the sun, shining all around me and those who were journeying with me. And when we had all fallen to the ground, I heard a voice saying to me in the Hebrew dialect, 'Saul, Saul, why are you persecuting Me? It is hard for you to kick against the goads.' And I said, 'Who are You, Lord?' And the Lord said, 'I am Jesus whom you are persecuting. But get up and stand on your feet; for this purpose I have appeared to you, to appoint you a minister and a witness not only to the things which you have seen, but also to the things in which I will appear to you; rescuing you from the *Jewish* people and from the Gentiles, to whom I am sending you, to open their eyes so that they may turn from darkness to light and from the dominion of Satan to God, that they may receive forgiveness of sins and an inheritance among those who have been sanctified by faith in Me." (Acts 26:12–18)

Paul did not volunteer to become a minister of Jesus Christ; he was appointed one by the Lord Himself. Blinded and terrified by the majesty of Christ's glorious appearance, all he could say was "What shall I do, Lord?" (Acts 22:10).

Paul often stressed the marvelous fact that God had chosen him for the ministry. To the Romans he wrote that he was a minister to the Gentiles because of God's gracious choice of him: "I have written very boldly to you on some points so as to remind you again, because of the grace that was given me from God, to be a minister of Christ Jesus to the Gentiles, ministering as a priest the gospel of God, so that *my* offering of the Gentiles may become acceptable, sanctified by the Holy Spirit" (Rom 15:15–16). He was eager to affirm that it was God who gave him the ministry of reconciliation (2 Cor 5:18) and put him into the service of Jesus Christ (1 Tim 1:12). He said to Timothy, "There is one God, *and* one mediator also between God and men, *the* man Christ Jesus, who gave Himself as a ransom for all, the testimony *given* at the proper time. For this I was appointed a preacher and an apostle (I am telling the truth, I am not lying) as a teacher of the Gentiles in faith and truth" (1 Tim 2:5–7; cf. 2 Tim 1:11).

All Christians have been called to serve God in one capacity or another. As God is sovereign in calling men to salvation, so is He in calling them to service. The Holy Spirit gives spiritual gifts, which are enablements for the service to which one is called, according to His sovereign will (1 Cor 12:11). Like Paul, the believer's responsibility is to be obedient to that calling (Acts 26:19).

Because he was made a minister by sovereign call, Paul viewed his ministry as a **stewardship**

from God. Stewardship translates *oikonomia,* a compound word made up of *oikos* ("house") and *nemō* ("manage"). It means to manage a household as a steward of someone else's possessions. The steward had oversight of the other servants and handled the business and financial affairs of the household. That freed the owner to travel and pursue other interests. Being a steward was thus a position of great trust and responsibility in the ancient world.

Unlike many who have held high offices throughout the church's history, Paul sought no glory for himself. He wanted to be regarded "in this manner, as [a servant] of Christ and [a steward] of the mysteries of God. In this case, moreover, it is required of stewards that one be found trustworthy" (1 Cor 4:1–2). He had a God-given task that he was obligated to fulfill (cf. 1 Cor 9:16–17; Gal 2:7; Eph 3:2, 7–8). There is no stronger passage to show Paul's firm sense of the divine call in his life than 1 Corinthians 9:16–17. He writes, "If I preach the gospel, I have nothing to boast of, for I am under compulsion; for woe is me if I do not preach the gospel. For if I do this voluntarily, I have a reward; but if against my will, I have a stewardship entrusted to me." "I am under compulsion" is strong language. "Woe is me" is even stronger. He operated under the knowledge of a divine mandate that was not even voluntary initially. All who are called to preach should feel the compulsion, the fear of judgment, and the sense of stewardship Paul felt.

The church is the household of God (1 Tim 3:15), and all believers have the responsibility to manage the ministries the Lord has given them. Contrary to much popular teaching today, our spiritual gifts are not intended for our own edification. They are given to help us minister to others. Paul told the Colossians that his stewardship was **bestowed on me for your benefit.** Peter echoed the same truth when he wrote, "As each one has received a *special* gift, employ it in serving one another as good stewards of the manifold grace of God" (1 Pet 4:10). Leaders have a special stewardship: "The overseer must be above reproach as God's steward" (Titus 1:7). Every Christian will one day give account to Christ of his stewardship. May none of us be found poor stewards, like the lazy slave in the parable of the talents (Matt 25:24–25).

THE SPIRIT OF THE MINISTRY

Now I rejoice ... (1:24*a*)

As challenging and demanding as it is, ministry was never intended to be an arduous and unbearable burden. Paul's attitude of joy should be the spirit of ministry for every Christian. The sad reality is, however, that many Christians (even some pastors) have lost the joy of serving the Lord. They grudgingly carry out their responsibilities, with solemn faces and somber spirits. Like Jonah, they are hesitant, angry, bitter, and resentful. They are reminiscent of Elijah, who "requested for himself that he might die, and said, 'It is enough; now, O Lord, take my life, for I am not better than my fathers'" (1 Kgs 19:4).

The writer of Hebrews rebukes those pseudo-martyrs in no uncertain terms. He reminds them of "Jesus, the author and perfecter of faith, who for the joy set before Him endured the cross, despising the shame, and has sat down at the right hand of the throne of God. For consider Him who has endured such hostility by sinners against Himself, so that you will not grow weary and lose heart" (Heb 12:2–3). Jesus never lost the joy of His ministry, even when faced with the terrible reality of the cross. And, unlike Him, most believers "have not yet resisted to the point of shedding blood" (v. 4). A Christian who has lost the joy of the ministry does not have bad circumstances, but bad connections. You do not lose the joy of serving Christ unless your communion with Him breaks down.

Christian joy is internal. Paul was sometimes discouraged by his circumstances, but he maintained his joy. He described himself as "afflicted in every way, but not crushed; perplexed, but not despairing; persecuted, but not forsaken; struck down, but not destroyed" (2 Cor 4:8–9). He knew "great sorrow and unceasing grief" (Rom 9:2) over the plight of unbelieving Israel. Whatever Paul's circumstances, he never lost his deep-seated confidence that God is in control.

Joy is generated by humility. People lose their joy when they become self-centered, thinking they deserve better circumstances or treatment than they are getting. That was never a problem for Paul. Like all of God's great servants, he was conscious of his unworthiness. Imprisoned in Rome, while other preachers got the glory, he wrote, "Christ is proclaimed; and in this I rejoice. Yes, and I will rejoice" (Phil 1:18). Facing the possibility of martyrdom, he wrote, "Even if I am being poured out as a drink offering upon the sacrifice and service of your faith, I rejoice and share my joy with you all" (Phil 2:17). Beaten and imprisoned in Philippi, he sang hymns of praise to God (Acts 16:25). Because he believed he deserved nothing, no circumstance could shake his joyous confidence that God was in control of his life (cf. Col 2:5; 1 Thess 2:19–20; Phlm 7).

The joy of the early church was a dramatic testimony to the world. The second-century apologist Aristides wrote to the Roman emperor Antonius Pius a description of Christians that said if any righteous person from among them passed from this world the Christians would rejoice and give thanks to God.

When a child was born to Christian parents, they would praise God. If it died in infancy, according to Aristides, the parents thanked God even more because the child would be one who had passed through the world without encountering sin. (See *The Apology of Aristides*, trans. Rendel Harris [London: Cambridge, 1893].)

Circumstances, people, and worry are the thieves that are eager to steal the joy of the ministry. Humility, devotion to Christ, and trust in God protect the joy that is Christ's legacy to every Christian (cf. John 15:11; 17:13).

THE SUFFERING OF THE MINISTRY

... in my sufferings for your sake, and in my flesh I do my share on behalf of His body, which is the church, in filling up what is lacking in Christ's afflictions. (1:24*b*)

To emphasize that joy is independent of circumstances, Paul tells the Colossians that he rejoices **in my sufferings for your sake. Sufferings** refers to his present imprisonment (Acts 28:16, 30), from which he wrote Colossians. Paul could rejoice despite his imprisonment because he always viewed himself as a prisoner of Jesus Christ, not the Roman Empire (cf. Phlm 1, 9, 23).

The early church considered it a privilege to suffer for the name of Christ. In Acts 5:41, the apostles "went on their way from the presence of the Council, rejoicing that they had been considered worthy to suffer shame for *His* name." To the Philippians Paul wrote, "To you it has been granted for Christ's sake, not only to believe in Him, but also to suffer for His sake" (Phil 1:29). Why was suffering a cause for joy? The New Testament suggests at least five reasons.

First, suffering brings believers closer to Christ. Paul wrote, "That I may know Him and the power of His resurrection and the fellowship of His sufferings" (Phil 3:10). Suffering in the cause of Christ yields the fruit of better understanding of what Jesus went through in His suffering.

Second, suffering assures the believer that he belongs to Christ. Jesus said, "If the world hates you, you know that it has hated Me before *it hated* you" (John 15:18). Because "a disciple is not above his teacher, nor a slave above his master" (Matt 10:24), we will suffer. Paul warned Timothy, "Indeed, all who desire to live godly in Christ Jesus will be persecuted" (2 Tim 3:12). Peter tells suffering Christians, "If you are reviled for the name of Christ, you are blessed, because the Spirit of glory and of God rests on you" (1 Pet 4:14). Suffering causes believers to sense the presence of the Holy Spirit in their lives, which gives assurance of salvation.

Third, suffering brings a future reward. "If indeed we suffer with [Christ] so that we may also be glorified with *Him*. For I consider that the sufferings of this present time are not worthy to be compared with the glory that is to be revealed to us" (Rom 8:17–18). "For momentary, light affliction is producing for us an eternal weight of glory far beyond all comparison" (2 Cor 4:17).

Fourth, suffering can result in the salvation of others. Church history is filled with accounts of those who came to Christ after watching other Christians endure suffering.

Fifth, suffering frustrates Satan. He wants suffering to harm us, but God brings good out of it.

The statement **in my flesh I do my share on behalf of His body, which is the church, in filling up what is lacking in Christ's afflictions** has been the subject of much controversy. Roman Catholics have imagined here a reference to the suffering of Christians in purgatory. Christ's suffering, they maintain, was not enough to purge us completely from our sins. Christians must make up what was lacking in Christ's suffering on their behalf by their own suffering after death. That can hardly be Paul's point, however. He has just finished demonstrating that Christ alone is sufficient to reconcile us to God (1:20–23). To do an about face now and teach that believers must help pay for their sins would undermine his whole argument. The New Testament is clear that Christ's sufferings need nothing added to them. In Jesus' death on the cross, the work of salvation was completed. Further, the Colossian heretics taught that human works were necessary for salvation. To teach that believers' suffering was necessary to help expiate their sins would be to play right into the errorists' hands. The idea that Paul refers to suffering in purgatory is ruled out by both the general content of the epistle and the immediate context, as well as the obvious absence of any mention of a place like purgatory in Scripture. Finally, *thlipsis* (**afflictions**) is used nowhere in the New Testament to speak of Christ's sufferings.

In my flesh refers to Paul's physical pain. When he says **I do my share on behalf of His body, which is the church,** he is indicating that the physical pain he endures at the hands of Christ-hating persecutors is the result of what he does to benefit and build the church. It was not his personality that offended and brought hostile injury to him, but his ministry for the Body of Christ.

In what sense were Paul's sufferings **filling up what is lacking in Christ's afflictions?** In that Paul was receiving the persecution that was intended for Christ. Jesus, having ascended to heaven, was out of their reach. But because His enemies had not filled up all the injuries they wanted to inflict on Him, they turned their hatred on those who preached the gospel. It was in that sense that Paul filled up what was lacking in Christ's afflictions. In 2 Corinthians 1:5 he wrote that "the sufferings of Christ are ours in abundance." He bore in his body the marks of the blows intended for Christ (Gal 6:17; cf. 2 Cor 11:23–28). He not only suffered for Christ, but also for the sake of the church (2 Tim 2:10). Those who wish to represent Christ and serve His church must be willing to suffer for His Name.

THE SCOPE OF THE MINISTRY

... so that I might fully carry out the *preaching of* the word of God ... (1:25*b*)

Paul was driven to fulfill his ministry. He told the Ephesian elders, "I do not consider my life of any account as dear to myself, so that I may finish my course and the ministry which I received from the Lord Jesus, to testify solemnly of the gospel of the grace of God" (Acts 20:24). That ministry consisted primarily of **the *preaching of* the word of God,** of "declaring ... the whole purpose of God" (Acts 20:27). And Paul fulfilled that ministry. Near the end of his life he exclaimed triumphantly, "I have fought the good fight, I have finished the course, I have kept the faith" (2 Tim 4:7). His economy of effort, his single-minded devotion, and clear, direct focus on the task God had given him enabled him to carry out his ministry fully. He set himself to do God's will, nothing more or less, and stayed within that narrow prescription. He desired to preach the whole counsel of God to those to whom God called him, never shirking his duty or mitigating the divine message.

Some in the Lord's service think they have to win the entire world. As a result, they spread themselves so thin that they accomplish little. Paul was led by the Holy Spirit to make only three missionary journeys, all to the same general area. Yet few people in history have affected the world the way he did. Jesus never left Palestine, yet no one has come remotely close to having the impact on the world that He has. Jesus' ministry was effective because He limited it to doing what God wanted.

First, Jesus limited His ministry to God's will. He said in John 5:30, "I do not seek My own will, but the will of Him who sent Me." Too many men in the ministry are busy building their own empires, rather than seeking to fulfill God's will.

Second, Jesus limited His ministry to God's timing. The gospel of John repeatedly speaks of Jesus' hour as having not yet come (cf. 2:4; 7:30; 8:20; 12:27; 13:1; 17:1). Jesus carried out His ministry conscious of God's timing. He refused to do things until the right time.

Third, Jesus limited His ministry to God's objective. He knew that God had not sent Him to reach the entire world by Himself. In Matthew 15:24 He said, "I was sent only to the lost sheep of the house of Israel."

Fourth, Jesus limited His ministry to God's kingdom. He refused to be drawn into the political controversies of His day. When His opponents tried to embroil Him in one such controversy, He replied, "Render to Caesar the things that are Caesar's; and to God the things that are God's" (Matt 22:21). He kept the political realm and the spiritual realm separate. That is a lesson many in the contemporary church seem to have missed.

Fifth, Jesus limited Himself to God's people. He realized He could pour His life into only a few men. Out of the larger group of His followers, He chose the twelve and spent most of His time with them. And even among the twelve, He spent more time with Peter, James, and John than with the rest.

Those who desire truly effective ministries must learn the importance of limits. If they concentrate on the depth of their ministries, God will take care of the breadth.

THE SUBJECT OF THE MINISTRY

... ***that is,*** **the mystery which has been hidden from the** ***past*** **ages and generations, but has now been manifested to His saints, to whom God willed to make known what is the riches of the glory of this mystery among the Gentiles, which is Christ in you, the hope of glory.** (1:26–27)

The message Paul proclaimed in his ministry was **the mystery which has been hidden from the** ***past*** **ages and generations, but has now been manifested to His saints.** There are some things God reveals to no one. Deuteronomy 29:29 says, "The secret things belong to the LORD our God." God reveals other things only to certain people. "The secret of the LORD is for those who fear Him" (Ps 25:14). Proverbs 3:32 says, "He is intimate with the upright." Still other things were hidden in the Old Testament but have now been revealed in the New. The New Testament calls them mysteries (*mustērion*). Paul's use of this word is not to indicate a secret teaching, rite, or ceremony revealed only to some elite initiates (as in the mystery religions), but truth revealed to all believers in the New Testament. This truth, that has now **been manifested to His saints,** is that **which has been hidden from the** ***past*** **ages and generations,** namely the Old Testament era and people. **Now** refers to the time of the writing of the New Testament. Such newly revealed truth includes the mystery of the incarnate God (Col 2:2–3, 9); of Israel's unbelief (Rom 11:25); of lawlessness (2 Thess 2:7; cf. Rev 17:5, 7); of the unity of Jew and Gentile in the church (Eph 3:3–6); and of the rapture (1 Cor 15:51). This mystery truth is available only for those who are saints—true believers (cf. 1 Cor 2:7–16). The phrase **to whom God willed to make known** clearly indicates that the mysteries are not discovered by the genius of man, but are revealed by the will and act of God. It is God's purpose that His people know this truth.

Of all the mysteries God has revealed in the New Testament, the most profound is **Christ in you, the hope of glory.** The Old Testament predicted the coming of the Messiah. But the idea that He would actually live in His redeemed church, made up mostly of Gentiles, was not revealed. The New Testament is clear that Christ, by the Holy Spirit, takes up permanent residence in all believers (cf. Rom 8:9; 1 Cor 6:19, 20; Eph 2:22). The revelation of the riches of the glory of this mystery among the Gentiles awaited the New Testament (Eph 3:3–6). Believers, both Jew and Gentile, now possess the surpassing riches of the indwelling Christ (John 14:23; Rom 8:9–10; Gal 2:20; Eph 1:7, 17–18; 3:8–10, 16–19; Phil 4:19). The church is described as "the temple of the living God; just as God said, 'I WILL DWELL IN THEM AND WALK AMONG THEM; AND I WILL BE THEIR GOD, AND THEY SHALL BE MY PEOPLE'" (2 Cor 6:16). That Christ indwells all believers is the source for their **hope of glory** and is the subject or theme of the gospel ministry. What makes the gospel attractive is not just that it promises present joy and help, but that it promises eternal honor, blessing, and glory. When Christ comes to live in a believer, His presence is the anchor of the promise of heaven—the guarantee of future bliss eternally (cf. 2 Cor 5:1–5; Eph 1:13–14). In the reality that Christ is living in the Christian is the experience of new life and hope of eternal glory.

THE STYLE OF THE MINISTRY

We proclaim Him, admonishing every man and teaching every man with all wisdom ... (1:28*a*)

Paul's passion was to **proclaim Him** who had done so much for him. *Katangellō* (**proclaim**) means to publicly declare a completed truth or happening. It is a general term and is not restricted to formal preaching. Paul's proclamation included two aspects, one negative, one positive.

Admonishing is from *noutheteō*. It speaks of encouraging counsel in view of sin and coming punishment. It is the responsibility of church leaders. In Acts 20:31, Paul described his ministry at Ephesus: "Night and day for a period of three years I did not cease to admonish each one with tears." But it is also the responsibility of every believer. Paul wrote to the Thessalonians, "If anyone does not obey our instruction in this letter, take special note of that person and do not associate with him, so that he will be put to shame. *Yet* do not regard him as an enemy, but admonish him as a brother" (2 Thess 3:14–15).

Colossians 3:16 commands, "Let the word of Christ richly dwell within you, with all wisdom teaching and admonishing one another." Paul expressed his confidence that the Romans were "full of goodness, filled with all knowledge and able also to admonish one another" (Rom 15:14). If there is sin in the life of a believer, other believers have the responsibility to lovingly, gently admonish them to forsake that sin.

Teaching refers to imparting positive truth. It, too, is the responsibility of every believer (Col 3:16), and is part of the Great Commission (Matt 28:20). It is especially the responsibility of church leaders. "An overseer, then, must be ... able to teach" (1 Tim 3:2).

Admonishing and teaching must be done **with all wisdom.** This is the larger context. As discussed in chapter 2, **wisdom** refers to practical discernment—understanding the biblical principles for holy conduct. The consistent pattern of Paul's ministry was to link teaching and admonishment and bring them together in the context of the general doctrinal truths of the Word. Doctrinal teaching was invariably followed by practical admonitions. That must also be the pattern for all ministries.

THE SUM OF THE MINISTRY

... so that we may present every man complete in Christ. (1:28*b*)

The goal of the ministry is the maturity of the saints. Paul expressed that clearly in Ephesians 4:11–13: "[Christ] gave some *as* apostles, and some *as* prophets, and some *as* evangelists, and some *as* pastors and teachers, for the equipping of the saints for the work of service, to the building up of the body of Christ; until we all attain to the unity of the faith, and of the knowledge of the Son of God, to a mature man, to the measure of the stature which belongs to the fullness of Christ." That goal was shared by Epaphras, the founder of the Colossian church: "Epaphras, who is one of your number, a bondslave of Jesus Christ, sends you his greetings, always laboring earnestly for you in his prayers, that you may stand perfect and fully assured in all the will of God" (Col 4:12). Our aim is not merely to win people to Christ, but to bring them to spiritual maturity. They will then be able to reproduce their faith in others. In 2 Timothy 2:2 Paul charged Timothy, "The things which you have heard from me in the presence of many witnesses, entrust these to faithful men who will be able to teach others also."

To be **complete,** or mature, is to be like Christ. Although all Christians strive for that lofty end, no one on earth has arrived there yet (cf. Phil 3:12). Every believer, however, will one day attain it. "Beloved, now we are children of God, and it has not appeared as yet what we will be. We know that when He appears, we will be like Him, because we will see Him just as He is" (1 John 3:2). Christians move toward maturity by feeding on God's Word: "All Scripture is inspired by God and profitable for teaching, for reproof, for correction, for training in righteousness; so that the man of God may be adequate, equipped for every good work" (2 Tim 3:16–17).

The Colossian heretics believed perfection was only for the elite, a view shared by many others throughout history. The American journalist Walter Lippmann wrote,

> [As] yet, no teacher has ever appeared who was wise enough to know how to teach his wisdom to all mankind. In fact, the great teachers have attempted nothing so utopian. They were quite well aware how difficult for most men is wisdom, and they have confessedly stated that the perfect life was for the select few. (Walter Lippmann, *A Preface to Morals*, [New York: Macmillan, 1929], 199)

In contrast, Christ offers spiritual maturity to every man and woman.

THE STRENGTH OF THE MINISTRY

For this purpose also I labor, striving according to His power, which mightily works within me. (1:29)

Kopiaō (**labor**) means to work to the point of exhaustion. People sometimes tell me that I work too hard. But compared to Paul, I am not working hard enough. It saddens me to hear of pastors or seminary students who are looking for an easy pastorate. When I was a young pastor, a lady (who did not know I was a pastor) advised me to go into the ministry. When I asked her why, she replied that ministers did not have to do anything and could make lots of money.

No one would get that idea by observing Paul. Concerning those who denigrated his ministry, he wrote:

> Are they servants of Christ?—I speak as if insane—I more so; in far more labors, in far more imprisonments, beaten times without number, often in danger of death. Five times I received from the Jews thirty-nine *lashes*. Three times I was beaten with rods, once I was stoned, three times I was shipwrecked, a night and a day I have spent in the deep. *I have been* on frequent journeys, in dangers from rivers, dangers from robbers, dangers from *my* countrymen,

> dangers from the Gentiles, dangers in the city, dangers in the wilderness, dangers on the sea, dangers among false brethren; *I have been* in labor and hardship, through many sleepless nights, in hunger and thirst, often without food, in cold and exposure. Apart from *such* external things, there is the daily pressure on me *of* concern for all the churches. (2 Cor 11:23–28)

No one can successfully serve Jesus Christ without working hard. Lazy pastors, Christian leaders, or laymen will never fulfill the ministry the Lord has called them to. **Striving** is from *agōnizomai,* which refers to competing in an athletic event. Our English word *agonize* is derived from it. Success in serving the Lord, like success in sports, demands maximum effort.

Lest anyone misunderstand him, Paul says that he strives **according to His power, which mightily works within me.** All his toil and hard labor would have been useless apart from God's power in his life. To the Corinthians he wrote, "By the grace of God I am what I am, and His grace toward me did not prove vain; but I labored even more than all of them, yet not I, but the grace of God with me" (1 Cor 15:10). God gave Paul the strength to work hard at his ministry. Galatians 2:20 really sums up the two components in this human-divine action: "I have been crucified with Christ; and it is no longer I who live, but Christ lives in me; and the *life* which I now live in the flesh I live by faith in the Son of God, who loved me and gave Himself up for me."

These eight aspects of Paul's ministry should characterize every believer. All Christians serve Christ in some capacity. Paul's message to all in this passage is, "The things you have learned and received and heard and seen in me, practice these things" (Phil 4:9).

BIBLIOGRAPHY

Abbott, T. K. *A Critical and Exegetical Commentary on the Epistles to the Ephesians and to the Colossians.* Edinburgh: T & T Clark, 1985.

Barclay, William. *The Letters to the Philippians, Colossians, and Thessalonians.* Rev. ed. Philadelphia: Westminster, 1975.

———. *The Letters to Timothy, Titus, and Philemon.* Rev. ed. Philadelphia: Westminster, 1975.

Barnes, Albert. *Barnes' Notes on the Old & New Testaments: Ephesians, Philippians, and Colossians.* Grand Rapids: Baker, 1974.

———. *Barnes' Notes on the Old & New Testaments: Thessalonians, Timothy, Titus and Philemon.* Grand Rapids: Baker, 1975.

Barrett, William. *Irrational Man.* Garden City, NY: Doubleday, 1962.

Bruce, F. F. *The Epistles to the Colossians, to Philemon, and to the Ephesians.* Grand Rapids: Eerdmans, 1984.

Carson, Herbert M. *The Epistles of Paul to the Colossians and Philemon*. Grand Rapids: Eerdmans, 1982.

Chesnut, D. Lee. *The Atom Speaks*. San Diego: Creation-Science Research Center, 1973.

Dana, H. E., and Julius R. Mantey. *A Manual Grammar of the Greek New Testament*. New York: Macmillan, 1927.

DeYoung, Donald B. "Design in Nature: The Anthropic Principle." *Impact* 149 (November 1985).

Eadie, John. *A Commentary on the Greek Text of the Epistle of Paul to the Colossians*. Reprint. Grand Rapids: Baker, 1979.

Erdman, Charles R. *The Epistles of Paul to the Colossians and to Philemon*. Philadelphia: Westminster, 1966.

Gromacki, Robert G. *Stand Perfect in Wisdom: An Exposition of Colossians and Philemon*. Grand Rapids: Baker, 1981.

Guiness, Os. *The Dust of Death*. Downers Grove, IL: InterVarsity, 1973.

Guthrie, Donald. *New Testament Introduction*. Downers Grove, IL: InterVarsity, 1970.

Harrison, Everett F. *Colossians: Christ All-Sufficient*. Chicago: Moody, 1971.

Hendriksen, William. *Philippians, Colossians and Philemon*. Grand Rapids: Baker, 1964.

Henry, Matthew. *Matthew Henry's Commentary on the Whole Bible*. Vol. 6. Old Tappan, NJ: Revell, n.d.

Ironside, H. A. *Lectures on the Epistle to the Colossians.* New York: Loizeaux, 1928.

Jastrow, Robert, and Malcolm H. Thompson. *Astronomy: Fundamentals and Frontiers.* New York: John Wiley & Sons, 1977.

Kent, Homer A. *Treasures of Wisdom: Studies in Colossians & Philemon.* Grand Rapids: Baker, 1978.

Lenski, R. C. H. *The Interpretation of St. Paul's Epistles to the Colossians, to the Thessalonians, to Timothy, to Titus and to Philemon.* Minneapolis: Augsburg, 1946.

Lightfoot, J. B. *St. Paul's Epistles to the Colossians and to Philemon.* 1879. Reprint. Grand Rapids: Zondervan, 1959.

Lippmann, Walter. *A Preface to Morals.* New York: Macmillan, 1929.

Maclaren, Alexander. *The Epistles of St. Paul to the Colossians and Philemon.* New York: A. C. Armstrong and Son, 1903.

Morris, Henry M. *The Biblical Basis for Modern Science.* Grand Rapids: Baker, 1984.

Moule, H. C. G. *Colossian Studies.* New York: Hodder and Stoughton, n.d.

Nieder, John, and Thomas Thompson. *Forgive and Love Again.* Eugene, OR: Harvest House, 1991.

Richardson, Cyril C. *Early Christian Fathers.* New York: Macmillan, 1978.

Rienecker, Fritz, and Cleon Rogers. *Linguistic Key to the Greek New Testament.* Grand Rapids: Zondervan, 1982.

Robertson, A. T. *Word Pictures in the New Testament.* Vol. 4, The Epistles of Paul. Nashville: Broadman, 1931.

Rosenberger, Donald A. "What Happened to the Man Who Led the Attack on Pearl Harbor?" *Command,* Fall/Winter, 1991.

Rupprecht, Arthur A. "Philemon." In *The Expositor's Bible Commentary,* vol. 11. Grand Rapids: Zondervan, 1978.

Schaeffer, Francis. *Escape from Reason.* Downers Grove, IL: InterVarsity, 1972.

———. *He Is There and He Is Not Silent.* Wheaton, IL: Tyndale, 1972.

———. *The God Who Is There.* Downers Grove, IL: InterVarsity, 1968.

Schlatter, Adolf. *The Church in the New Testament Period.* London: SPCK, 1955.

Smith, M. A. *From Christ to Constantine.* Downers Grove, IL: InterVarsity, 1973.

Vaughan, Curtis. "Colossians." In *The Expositor's Bible Commentary,* vol. 11. Grand Rapids: Zondervan, 1978.

Vincent, Marvin R. *Word Studies in the New Testament.* Vol. 3, The Epistles of Paul. New York: Scribner's, 1904.

Vine, W. E. *An Expository Dictionary of New Testament Words*. Old Tappan, NJ: Revell, 1966.

Wuest, Kenneth S. *Wuest's Word Studies from the Greek New Testament*. Vol. 1. Grand Rapids: Eerdmans, 1973.

INDEXES

INDEX OF SCRIPTURE

INDEX OF SUBJECTS

JOHN MACARTHUR PUBLISHING GROUP
LOS ANGELES, CALIFORNIA